YOURS VERY S

Letters from Fergus Macdonald

CONTENTS

INTRODUCTION

These letters (and three reports) were written over a four year period while Fergus Macdonald was General Secretary of the United Bible Societies. More or less at the mid-point of that period (October 2000) the UBS World Assembly took place in Midrand, South Africa. The World Assembly is a unique and colourful occasion taking place roughly every four years when all the UBS member Bible Societies are represented. In addition to determining broad strategic directions of the UBS for the following four years, World Assemblies are great occasions of inspiration, cross-cultural learning, building trust, mutual encouragement. It is because their effectiveness depends on thorough preparation and creative follow-up that there are frequent references in these letters to Midrand. References to Mississauga relate to the 1996 World Assembly.

Although the letters are set in a Bible Society context, non-Bible Society readers will readily be able to apply their message to their own situation.

British Library Cataloguing in Publication Data:
A catalogue record for this publication
is available from the British Library

ISBN   1 871828 52 X

© **The Handsel Press 2004**
62 Toll Rd
Kincardine
FK10 4QZ
Scotland

Typeset in 11 pt. Garamond

Printed by Polestar Wheatons Ltd, Aberdeen

Stocked and distributed by the Scottish Bible Society
7 Hampton Terrace, Edinburgh EH12 5XU

YEAR ONE

February 1998 MOVEMENT OR INSTITUTION?

A Happy New Year! Yes, I know it's now February, but Scots have always asserted the right to celebrate the New Year much longer than others! So please allow me to take this opportunity to wish all of you God's richest blessings throughout 1998. May it be a year in which the power of the Holy Spirit activates the Scriptures you translate, distribute and promote in such a way that the churches we serve grow, multiply and glorify God!

First of all, I would like to say `thank you' to the Fellowship for appointing me as General Secretary of the United Bible Societies. This is a great honour for me and I am really excited by the many opportunities facing us in our mission as a fellowship. I pray that, under God, I may prove worthy of the trust you have placed in me.

Second, allow me to say `please'! Please continue to pray for me during the first months of this new ministry. I very much value your prayers and have been deeply moved by the large number of assurances of prayer and support received from all over our fellowship since my appointment was announced. This encourages me to ask you to continue praying that I may be granted divine wisdom and vision as I fulfil `routine' as well as `key' responsibilities.

Prayer, of course, is important for all aspects of our work as a family of Bible Societies. For the UBS' vital ministry of the Word will be accomplished effectively only if it is continually supported in prayer. We dare not attempt to fulfil our ministry carried along merely by the momentum of the past. We also need the dynamic of the Holy Spirit in the present which, astoundingly, Jesus says we simply have to ask for (Luke 11.13)!

We like to describe the UBS as a `movement' rather than an `institution'. This may not be quite accurate because there seems to be an unwritten law which says that no movement can survive only as a movement for the length of time many of our Bible Societies have been in existence. Inevitably movements become institutionalised to a greater or lesser extent as they develop by-laws, regulations, procedures etc – and the UBS is no exception.

At the same time, I am sure the deep desire of all of us is for the UBS to be more movement than institution! What can we do to help this to happen?

1

The answer is, of course, many things. But none of these is more important than praying! In God's economy, as we have seen, he pours out his Holy Spirit on those who ask. And we learn from the book of Acts how the Spirit provided vitality, purpose, creativity and energy to the early Christian community. And if to the early Christians, why not to us today?

The UBS is a *movement* to the degree to which we are open to being surprised by the Holy Spirit and carried along by him! And only if we are a movement will we have the flexibility to respond to his surprises!

So let us ask God for:
- Willingness to change
- A proactive mind-set
- A sanctified imagination
- A risk-taking faith
- A frontier spirit

and move forward together!

Let us make Paul's request to the Thessalonians a mutual request from and to us all:

> **Finally, our friends, please pray for us. This will help the message about the Lord to spread quickly, and others will respect it, just as you do.** (2 Thess 3.1, CEV)

March 1998   ENCOURAGEMENT

This month's letter was begun on the island of Cyprus during the biennial conference of General Secretaries from the Europe-Middle East region at which I was invited to give a presentation on the identity and ethos of the UBS.

One of the key components of our ethos was captured on the first day by our UBS Executive Committee chairman, Dr Eugene Habecker. He reminded us that Cyprus was the home of Barnabas, one of the early Christians who was so named by the apostles because he was `one who encourages others' (Acts 4.36).

During the conference, as at the World Assembly in Mississauga, I became very conscious that the UBS is essentially a fellowship. I am convinced that this is the key word in the current UBS statement of identity. It reads:

> The United Bible Societies is a world *fellowship* of Bible Societies, united for consultation, mutual support and action in the common task of achieving the widest possible effective distribution of the Holy Scriptures.

Being a fellowship, a key component of our UBS ethos must surely be to encourage one another. The New Testament word for fellowship – *koinonia* – means partnership. And one of the key assets each of us brings to our UBS partnership is mutual encouragement.

Each of the four days of the conference began with a dramatised Bible reading from 1 Thessalonians in the Contemporary English Version (CEV) followed by group discussion. In these groups we soon discovered a strong link between 1 Thessalonians and Barnabas, for this letter is essentially a message of encouragement.

As the comprehensive programme of the conference unfolded, the relevance of this letter to the life of our UBS family came home to me in a new way. Let me share with you some of my reflections. I came to realise that the `mutual support' in our identity statement is the gift, the task and the privilege of encouraging one another, just as much as sharing financial and personnel resources. In the light of this, I found 1 Thessalonians has three important things to say to all of us.

Spirituality

First, it indicates that the *motive* for encouraging one another arises from a deep spirituality. Christian spirituality is the fruit of the Holy Spirit working in our lives. `Don't turn away God's Spirit' (CEV) or `Do not put out the Spirit's fire' (NIV) – compare 1.5-6, 4.8, 5.19.

In the Bible study groups in Cyprus we heard personal testimonies from colleagues living in the Middle East and the former Communist world of how the Holy Spirit had made them glad even when they suffered (1.6), how they were able to adopt a `eucharistic life style' by thanking God whatever happened (5.18).

Sincerity

Second, 1 Thessalonians makes clear that the *mode* of mutual encouragement is true sincerity. Chapter 2 rings with Paul's sincerity as he recalls his relationship with the Thessalonians on his visit to their city:

-   We didn't try to fool or trick anyone (2.3)
-   We didn't speak to please people, but to please God (2.4)
-   We didn't try to flatter anyone (2.5)
-   What we did was not a cover-up for greed (2.5)
-   We were pure and honest and innocent in our dealings with you (2.10)

3

There was an open transparency about Paul which enabled the Thessalonians to accept his encouragement at its face value. They didn't suspect any subtle attempt to manipulate simply because it didn't exist.

The Latin root of `sincerity' is *sine cera,* i.e. without wax. In the ancient world some makers of marble statues and ornaments would cleverly conceal cavities in the marble by filling them with wax coloured to match the stone. So before making a purchase, vendors were often asked to place items for sale in the hot sun. In this way any wax would melt and hidden defects be revealed. Only the pieces of marble which stood the test and proved to be *sine cera* were considered genuine.

One of the most encouraging features of the Cyprus conference was the transparency and openness of the discussions which made it easy for participants to encourage one another. This relaxed openness enabled each one to be a Barnabas to the others.

Solidarity

Third, 1 Thessalonians describes the *manifestation* of encouragement. This manifestation is practical solidarity among the members of the fellowship. We see this solidarity, first of all, between Paul, Silas and Timothy and the Thessalonian believers:

- We were eager to see you and tried our best to visit you in person. We really wanted to come (2.17)
- You want to see us as much as we want to see you (3.6)

Many of the General Secretaries in Europe and the Middle East will echo these words as they look back on Cyprus, just as their counterparts in the Americas, Africa and Asia look back on similar events in Guatemala, in Johannesburg and in Thailand.

But of course, good memories are not enough! Solidarity must be worked at! Encouraging one another is also a present and a future activity. As we seek to maintain a network of mutual support and concern right across our global family, Paul's advice to us through the Thessalonians is well worth following:

- Try to get along with each other (5.13)
- Encourage anyone who feels left out (5.14)
- Help all who are weak (5.14)
- Be patient with everyone (5.14)

Encouraging one another! Its motivation, its mode and its manifestation are all there in this ancient letter to a fledgling church.

So let us all work together to make the UBS an 'Order of Barnabas'! Let us follow his example and encourage others. And by so doing may we, like him, be seen to be good people, of great faith and filled with the Holy Spirit, and become effective in the service of the Word of God (Acts 11.24)!

We thank God for you and always mention you in our prayers. Each time we pray, we tell God our Father about your faith and loving work and about your firm hope in our Lord Jesus Christ. (1 Thess 1.2-3)

April 1998   NIAGARA FALLS

A few weeks ago I had the opportunity to re-visit the Niagara Falls on the Canadian-United States border. This visit was made in the depths of the Canadian winter: the river banks were snow covered and enormous icicles hung from the cliffs next to the falls. After dark, powerful lights illuminated the cascading water in a brilliant variety of colours filtered by the rising spray.

My previous visit, made some years ago, was in high summer, when conditions were very different: the stronger natural colours and higher temperatures seemed to soften – just a little – the foaming outburst of nature's raw energy. The long summer day meant that I had left before the illuminations were switched on. But on both occasions the overwhelming impact – of the enormous power of flowing, falling water in great volume – was the same. This time, like the last, I stood and gazed in awe at the enormous manifestation of natural might called Niagara.

Reflecting on this visit, it struck me that Niagara is a striking image of spiritual power. After all, in Scripture water is a symbol of the Holy Spirit: 'On the last and most important day of the festival, Jesus stood up and shouted, "If you are thirsty, come to me and drink! Have faith in me, and you will have life-giving water flowing from deep inside you, just as the Scriptures say." Jesus was talking about the Holy Spirit, who would be given to everyone that had faith in him' (John 7.37-39).

The Scriptures teach that above all else the Holy Spirit empowers: 'God's Spirit does not make cowards out of us. The Spirit gives us power, love and self-control' (2 Tim 1.7).

And it is the Holy Spirit who raised Jesus from death (Romans 1.4). This Easter we are reminded both that the power of the risen Christ was demonstrated in a unique past event, and also that it is a power which, like Niagara, continues day after day. `I want you to know about the great and mighty power that God has for us followers. It is the same wonderful power he used when he raised Christ from death and let him sit at his right side in heaven. There Christ rules....' (Eph 1.19-20). The same tide that lifts the small row boat lifts the world's largest super-tanker!

May Easter 1998 help us all to discover more of this divine power in our personal and family lives, as well as in our service to the Bible cause!

Finally, here is another biblical metaphor. Ezekiel had a powerful vision of a trickle of water flowing from under the threshold of the Jerusalem temple in ever growing volume until it becomes a mighty torrent, plunging down a series of wadis into the Jordan rift valley 4,000 feet below, bringing life to the barren desert and turning the salty Dead Sea into a fresh water lake teeming with fish! Ezekiel's interpreter captured the message of the vision in one terse phrase: **`So where the water flows everything will live.'** (Ezekiel 47.9)

May 1998   BURDENS

One of the best known sayings of Jesus is: `If you are tired from carrying heavy burdens, come to me and I will give you rest'. (Matt 11.28, CEV)

These famous words appear in many Bible Society selections designed as evangelistic tools for the churches to use in programmes of mission. This of course is perfectly appropriate since Jesus' original audience was people who were so crushed under a plethora of religious regulations laid upon them by their leaders that their faith had become for them a burden rather than a blessing. Jesus' saying remains totally relevant for all who find the demands of moral and religious duty unsustainable.

But it seems to me that these words of Jesus also have a message for us inside the Bible Society movement. Is it not the case that many of us who serve as staff and Board members are finding that there are times when our work for the Bible cause is a heavy burden? Indeed, the exhaustion which this causes can be so great that we lose our creativity and our cutting edge! This is by no means a problem unique to Bible Society people. It is also true of many other Christian workers today; terms like `stress' and `burn-out' are commonplace in the vocabulary of many churches.

When the load becomes too great!

When this happens, our 'work' in the Bible cause becomes just as oppressive as the 'works' which Jesus' contemporaries found so burdensome! So when the load in the office or on the Board or on UBS committees becomes too great, Matthew 11.28-30 becomes a word of the Lord for us!

The implication is that periodically it's good for us to hand over our work to Christ. After all, he offers to carry our burdens! Who better to handle the churches' headaches than the Head of the Church! This requires a conscious effort on our part – it doesn't happen automatically. But when we do it, Jesus promises to give us 'rest' i.e. relief.

Of course, it is important to remember that by giving us rest, Jesus does not free us from responsibility. For when we give him our burden, he then gives us his 'yoke'. 'Take the yoke I give you. Put it on your shoulders and learn from me' (v.29, CEV). I believe that the burden and the yoke are one and the same. What we hand over to him as our burden he returns to us as his yoke!

Lightening the burden!

But there is a great difference. 'This yoke is easy to bear, and this burden is light.' (v.30 CEV) What makes the difference? When the people came to Jesus burdened with myriads of detailed religious 'works', he took their burden and dramatically reduced it by doing two things:

- He identified 'the more important matters of the Law, such as justice, mercy and faithfulness'.

- He emphasised that the Law was essentially an expression of love: the two great commandments are to love God and to love our neighbour (Matt 22.34-40).

Similarly with us. When we bring our work and lay it at the feet of Jesus, acknowledging that it is his gift to us and that, therefore, it is his before it is ours, two things happen:

- We gain a new perspective which enables us to prioritise and concentrate on the essential tasks.

- We experience spiritual renewal so that what before was heavy is now light! We now see our life work as a made-to-measure task, just like a well-made ox yoke.

By learning from him, we discover work once again as a joy, not a burden. We do it out of love for Christ and for the world for which he died. We find that love makes even the heaviest load light.

William Barclay tells the story of a man who came upon a little boy carrying a still smaller boy, who was lame, on his back. 'That's a heavy burden for you to carry', said the man. 'That's not a burden', came the reply, 'that's my little brother!' Barclay's comment on the story is surely relevant to our theme: 'The burden which is given in love and carried in love is always light.'

There's an old Christian legend that Jesus the carpenter made the best ox yokes in Galilee.

June 1998   WORLD CUP

The big event this month for millions of people all over the world is the Soccer World Cup tournament which kicks off on 10 June with Brazil playing Scotland in the new Stade de France at St Denis on the northern outskirts of Paris. Soccer will rule the world's media for the four weeks of the competition and it is expected that the final on 12 July will be watched and/or heard by hundreds of millions of people.

World Cup Parable

We can see the World Cup as a modern parable of the UBS. Just as success in the competition depends on team work, commitment and coordination, so also our Bible Society service to the churches of the world becomes more effective when we as Bible Societies co-operate, build a common vision and coordinate the use of our limited resources.

Of course, the parable can also apply at the level of our national Bible Societies. Each Bible Society is a team - composed of Board and staff dedicated to achieving, under God, the effective distribution and use of the Holy Scriptures in their country and beyond.

If we watch the World Cup games on television, why don't we work out the lessons of this parable? One way of doing this would be to identify the factors contributing to the success of the winning teams. I'm sure you will find out that these include:

- *Commitment.* Playing well and winning come first. All other activities take second place to soccer!

- *Discipline.* Outstanding players achieve peak fitness through high personal discipline. This is never easy! The ancient Greeks used the word *agon* - from which our English word "agony" is derived - to describe their sporting events.

- *Team work.* The winning teams are composed of players who support each other, work together and resist the temptation to do their own thing.

- *Coordination.* This is more than inter-player cooperation. Successful teams are composed of players who skillfully coordinate eye, feet and head to make the ball go where they want it to go.

- *Concentration.* Great players are not distracted by the great numbers of noisy spectators around them. They concentrate on the game, not the onlookers.

World Cup Challenge

The World Cup represents an evangelistic opportunity. The French Bible Society is actively facing the challenge presented by the hundreds of thousands of soccer fans from France and many other countries who will pack the stadiums. The Bible Society has produced a special portion entitled `Gagner' (To win) containing 30 daily Bible readings and meditations. In addition, a subsidised slim-line New Testament is available for churches planning distribution during the competition. And the UBS Minorities Fund is providing 10,000 Arabic-French Testaments for free distribution among Arabic-speaking visitors.

In Brazil the Bible Society has produced a special World Cup edition of the Portuguese New Testament. There is also a promotional video - containing the testimonies of Christian players in the national team - which challenges churches in Brazil to see the massive interest in the World Cup as a unique opportunity to communicate God's Word.

In addition, Agape UK are making available a special edition of the JESUS video (a dramatisation of Luke's Gospel) for the World Cup called 'The Greatest Game - The Greatest Name'. A six-minute introduction contains endorsements for the video from three Brazilian team players including the goal keeper who saved the World Cup for Brazil in 1994.

The Goal that really matters!

One final reflection on the World Cup! St Paul talks about the one goal which ultimately matters more than any other: `I run towards the goal', he says (Philippians 3.14). Of course, he's thinking of a foot race rather than a football game - of a finishing line, not soccer goal posts!

And why did the apostle run towards the goal?

`So that I can win the prize of being called to heaven. This is the prize that God offers because of what Christ Jesus has done'. (CEV)

So the World Cup can be made a parable of life itself, not only of the UBS! This is the view of Claudio Andre Tafferel, one of the great stars in the Brazil team: `My greatest joy as a professional footballer was to win the World Cup in 1994,' he says in the introduction to *The Greatest Game - The Greatest Name*. `But after a few days, the memories began to fade away, as do all things in life. But my relationship with God will never fade away.'

Let's pray that many who play and watch the greatest game this month and next may learn through the World Cup Scripture distribution program to follow the greatest Name!

July 1998 CONSUMERS AND CITIZENS

I am sure that many of you who enjoy an American breakfast of bacon and egg will have heard of the farmyard conversation between the hen and the pig comparing their respective contributions to this traditional western meal. The hen boasted of her regular egg laying pattern.

`This means', she said, `that the average American can confidently walk into his restaurant every morning and know that his favourite breakfast is awaiting him.'

`But you forget one thing', responded the pig. `Your contribution to the breakfast may, indeed, be an offering. But mine is a total commitment!'

From commitment to consumption

This apocryphal story came to mind when reading *Fragmented Gods, the Poverty and Potential of Religion in Canada* by Reginald Bibby. This book highlights and documents the move away from religious commitment towards religious consumption which has overtaken not only Canada, but the entire western world, and is now beginning to threaten third world churches as well.

Bibby observes that churches are serving up religion in whatever form consumers want. He also claims that in Canada this is true not only of Christianity, but of all faiths. `They have not provided a religion based on what religion is, but a religion based on what the market will bear.'

What does this change of focus mean for Bible Societies?

The new mood has undoubtedly influenced us. The most obvious example is that we now take the market much more seriously than we once did. Increasingly we market our Scriptures in ways which underline their relevance to the felt needs of potential readers and hearers. And surely this is right. For Jesus met people where they were. He got inside their world before inviting them to enter his. The apostles followed his example. And they have left us the New Testament written, not in the classical Greek of the literati of the time, but in the common Greek of the market place.

From the market to the manger

However, there are other aspects of consumerism which we in the Bible Societies might do well to question. For example, focusing on felt needs alone can expose us to the charge of manipulation. It's important to remind ourselves that felt needs were the place where Jesus began. They were not where he ended. Having gained the interest and sympathy of his hearers, Jesus then moved on to help them identify deeper needs. In fact, we can say that again and again he moved on from relating to human needs to presenting divine claims. His dialogue with the woman of Samaria in John 4 is a case in point.

Since in Bible Society service Jesus is our ultimate model, our task is to communicate the Bible as a Word which both focuses on human needs and highlights divine claims. Through its words, God speaks his Word which both satisfies and startles us. We consume it as the living water for which we thirst; at the same time it confronts us as an ultimatum from heaven.

Because the 'market' is the place where non-church members are introduced to the Scriptures, Bible Societies must be adept at marketing. But marketing is not an end in itself. We help the Word to meet people where they are in order that it might lead them on from the market to the manger, to Calvary and to the empty tomb. For these are the places where people are confronted by the mighty deeds of God and are met by the One who can meet their deepest needs.

A final word on the best way to focus on consumption and commitment in promoting the Scriptures. Perhaps the key is for us in our personal use of the Bible to get the balance right between on the one hand being consumers of the Word as the bread and water of life, and on the other being citizens of the household of God, now and in the future (Eph 2.19, Phil 3.20). To return to the story of the hen and the pig: as consumers we make an offering, but as citizens we are asked to make a total commitment.

August 1998   IDOL OR ICON?

Some of you will know the parody of the famous hymn *Onward Christian Soldiers*. One of the verses goes like this:

> Like a mighty tortoise moves the Church of God,
> Brothers, we are treading where we've always trod!

To ensure that similar verses will never be composed about the UBS, our Fellowship is engaged in a process of interaction and reflection on our identity and ethos as a worldwide family of Bible Societies. It is intended that this process will culminate in the World Assembly to be held in October 2000, and its aim is to enable the UBS to enter the new millennium with a clearly focused vision and renewed commitment to fulfilling our mission.

In the 25 months between now and the Assembly all member Bible Societies will be invited to contribute to this dialogue. We are anxious that also individual Board members, staff (both Bible Society and UBS), volunteers and supporters become involved. The aim of this month's *For Your Information* is to encourage all of you to respond positively to invitations you will receive in the months ahead, expressing very frankly your thoughts on the identity and ethos of the UBS.

Alive and active

Such periodic identity renewal exercises are essential if any organisation is to remain alive and get to the cutting edge of its mission. Like the cells of the human body, corporate entities require regular inner renewal!

Your involvement is vital because this kind of renewal, to be successful, has to take place on the frontiers of an organisation, not in its back rooms. So let me say to those of you who live and work in translation, publishing and distribution, grappling with the challenges of new media and helping Scripture users to engage with the Good News: 'You *must* get involved!'

In the light of this process of consultation which lies ahead of us, I would like this month to share with you some reflections on *image*. Image and identity are not the same, but they are related. Our image is others' perception of our identity. This image may be true or it may be false. It may confirm our real identity in the eyes of others or it may distort, or even contradict, it. The image we seek to promote may not be the image which is perceived.

It's probably true to say that the concept of image has never been taken more seriously than it is today. Increasingly, people and organisations seem to live according to their image. Marshall McLuhan, the Canadian professor who popularised the phrase `the medium is the message', used to tell the story of a mother whose baby in arms was being much admired by onlookers. She responded by saying 'You should see his photo!'

> For better or for ill, image is pervading more and more of our lives. In politics style replaces substance. In commerce packaging and promotion replace quality. In society how you look replaces who you are.... The things that you say and do are all external, but the real you is lost. Like Madonna, you just live in the image.
>
> (Jock MacGregor of L'Abri Fellowship)

Relevant and real

In such a world the UBS and its member Bible Societies dare not underestimate the importance of image. It seems to me that the challenge facing us is two-fold: to be relevant and real at the same time.

The relevance challenge arises because there is always a temptation in a movement approaching its third century to become too focused in the past and thus gain an image of being caught in a time warp! Yet, at the same time, we dare not forget the past. Just as amnesia sufferers demonstrate that life without memory is meaningless, organisations without some conscious continuity with their past will tend to lose their sense of mission and, indeed, their identity. So the challenge is to be relevant while retaining our roots.

The other challenge is to be real! Relevance can sometimes be gained at the expense of ceasing to be real! A contemporary image is of little use if there is no reality behind it. Reality checks are vital! This challenge to be real is intensified in our media culture where images are constantly changing.

We are always looking for the new, always moving from one image to the next, changing to meet the pragmatic needs of the moment or discarding the old when it becomes boring, demanding or problematic (Jock MacGregor).

The problem is that people move on from the present image to the next before the present image matures. In the end life becomes almost a game. In fact, some contemporary western philosophers say it is a game! Organisations sometimes reflect a similar pattern, moving from one management fad to the next without providing sufficient opportunity for either to take root. They escape old age by being trapped in adolescence!

Icon and idol

The Bible has a clear message for us on images. It lays great stress on true image over against false image. The two main Greek biblical terms for image - *eidolon* and *eikon* - have come into other languages as `idol' and `icon'.

The New Testament use of both demonstrates how these words have very different meanings. Idols - although everywhere in vogue during the first century - are portrayed as being fraudulent and powerless without any real existence. (`No idol in the world really exists' - 1 Corinthians 8.4).

On the other hand, the term `icon' is very different. Far from being unreal, icon sums up the essence of the reality it represents. It is used to describe Jesus' relation to God (2 Cor 4.4; Col 1.15), and is closely associated with the Greek term *charakter* which has found its way into English as `character'. Apparently, a `character' was originally an embosser, a stamp for making coins, which in turn came to describe the image embossed on the coins because of the exact correspondence between the image and the device on the die.

This sharp biblical contrast between *idol* and *icon* suggests the need for reality checks when dealing with image, whether of individuals or organisations. An image can be true, or it can be false. On the whole Bible Societies and the UBS are highly regarded, i.e. they have a good image. But periodic reality checks are needed to ensure that internal reality confirms public image.

What, then, are some markers to help us make a reality check? I suggest three - not many, but perhaps enough for a beginning:

- View the past as a launch pad, not an arm chair

- Treat the present as a work place, not a playground

- Enter the future helping God to create it

Just as our UBS identity arises from the past, expresses itself in the present and is oriented to the future, so also a healthy, mature image will reflect past, present and future in the right proportions.

Finally, a word of wisdom from the Nineteenth Century Danish Christian philosopher, Soren Kierkegaard:

> `Life is lived forwards, but learned backwards.'

Last month I had a visit from Edwin Robertson, author of the UBS history, *Taking the Word to the World*, which was launched at the 1996 Mississauga World Assembly. Edwin is such a refreshing person - I am always left with sparkling new insights after talking with him!

On this particular occasion we were talking about the key role that the Psalms of the Old Testament could play in helping 21st century people to access the Word of God. A growing number of people today are embarking on a spiritual quest, but, sadly, so often they are passing the churches by! We concluded that perhaps one of the challenges we in the Bible Society movement face is to present the Psalms as the gateway into the Bible.

All of us find enormous spiritual resources in the Psalms, especially when we use them as prayers as well as a focus for meditation. Edwin Robertson shared with me his deep appreciation for Dietrich Bonhoeffer's booklet, *The Psalms: Prayer Book of the Bible*, which I immediately obtained and read avidly. I would like, if I may, this month to share with you a few of the gems I found in this little book.

Bonhoeffer very helpfully relates the use of the Psalms to learning to pray in the name of Jesus Christ. As we pray in the words of the Psalms, `It is always Jesus Christ we hear praying with us and ... we come with Jesus Christ in prayer before the throne of God.'

Bonhoeffer stresses the value of learning the Psalms and using them as prayers.

- `So if the Bible contains a book of prayers, we are to learn from this that the Word of God includes not only the words he wants to say to us, but also the words he wants to hear from us.'

- `What matters is not what we feel like praying about, but what God wants us to ask him for. Left to ourselves, no doubt we should often pray no more than the fourth petition of the Lord's Prayer.' (`Give us our daily bread').

The importance and relevance of the Psalms for us in the UBS at the present moment when we are re-thinking through our identity and ethos came home to me recently when I put together two texts. The first has been around for three millennia; the second for less than a decade. Here they are:

- `Then King David sat before the LORD, and prayed.' (2 Sam 7.18; 1 Chron 17.16)

- 'Where we stand depends on where we sit.' (Stephen Covey)

Stephen Covey, the American philosopher-guru, relates *ethos* to *pathos*. He tells us the ancient Greeks used *ethos* to describe personal integrity and credibility, while *pathos* for them was essentially feeling. Both formed a counterbalance to *logos*, the reasoning, logical approach. The strength of the Psalms is that they help us to develop spiritual pathos - to feel in a mysterious sense and to carry this sense of God with us into the world, making our ethos attractive and our logos convincing.

October 1998   SEED TO HARVEST

These words are being composed immediately following a visit to the beautiful city of Fredrikstad in southern Norway to attend the service of consecration as Bishop of Borg of Revd Ole Christian Kvarme, the former General Secretary of the Norwegian Bible Society. The service, held in the town's lovely 19th century cathedral, was most impressive and was marked by a deep sense of devotion and magnificent choral singing.

It was a privilege to represent the UBS at this event along with Eugene Habecker, Lucien Accad, Doron Even Ari and Gunnleik Seierstad. Also present were others with Bible Society connections, not least Rt Revd Andreas Aarflot, Chairman of the Norwegian Bible Society and the recently retired Bishop of Oslo, and Rt Revd Gunnar Stalsett, his successor as bishop and also a former General Secretary of the Bible Society.

Confidence and hope

All of us who were at the Mississauga Assembly will never forget Ole Kvarme's challenging presentation on *Bible Societies in the Third Millennium: The Challenge of the Global* Village in which he eloquently challenged our Fellowship to move into the new millennium, embracing its opportunities with confidence and hope. We wish him the Lord's richest blessing as he begins a new and vitally important ministry in his homeland.

16

Bishop Kvarme's consecration took place in the third week in September, by which time the grain harvest is normally complete in northern Europe. Yet I noticed a large proportion of the crops – oats, barley, wheat – were still standing in the fields. The Scandinavian summer has been so wet this year that the farmers were well behind.

Norwegian friends who answered my queries on this assured me that the harvest would in time be reaped. Certainly, during the two days I was in the country, the farmers could be seen taking advantage of a welcome spell of good weather, busy with their combine harvesters gathering in the standing grain.

`Is there a parable here for the us in the UBS?' I asked myself. We rightly think of the Word of God as seed (Matt 13.1-23) and focus on the beginning of the agricultural cycle in making biblical allusions to our work. Perhaps we need to balance this by reminding ourselves that the same Lord who said 'The seed is the word', saw the crowds around him as a large harvest, ripe and ready to be gathered in (Matthew 9.27)!

Seed and sickle

There is certainly a large harvest being reaped today. The recently published *Atlas of World Christianity* informs us that the net daily increase in the size of the total global Christian community is of the order of 50,000. Some of this is biological growth resulting from the high birth-rate in countries where churches are growing. But a significant part is conversion growth. Either way, the provision of the Word of God is vital if these new Christians are to become disciples. So there is a sense in which the Word of God fulfils the role of sickle as well as seed in helping the Kingdom of God to come.

The Atlas of World Christianity also informs us that the growth in the total Christian community, while still large and significant, is lower than it was in the eighties, when it averaged 68,000 per day. This raises an important question for us: is this reduction of over a quarter in the rate of Christian growth, related to our inability over the past ten years to meet the annual gap – which Ole Kvarme highlighted at Mississauga – of about US$30 million between the Scriptures requested and the Scriptures supplied from our World Service Program?

Shortfall and slowdown

Certainly, in the period of high growth between 1975 and 1985 David Barrett, editor of the World Christian Encyclopaedia, and others contended that there was a direct relation between the rate of Christian growth and the number of available Scriptures. So it is not unreasonable to deduce that the Scripture shortfall in the nineties is a major contributing factor to the slow down in the growth rate.

Other Bible agencies are also reporting a serious shortfall between the number of Scriptures needed and the number they are able to supply with limited financial resources.

There is of course a vital element of divine mystery in the growth of the church which we dare not overlook or underestimate. But William Carey taught us two centuries ago that God's sovereignty is consistent with the `use of means' – one of which is surely the translation and distribution of the Holy Scriptures.

Will church growth continue to slow down? Or will it, under God, take off again as we move into the third millennium? The answer probably depends on our success over the next few years in making the Scriptures available in sufficient languages, formats and quantities!

This underlines the vital importance of Bible work. Let us recommit ourselves to it so that the work of translation, distribution and use might become more effective than ever! Let us also redouble our efforts to inspire all our supporters to renew their vision of the vital importance of Bible work in the coming of the Kingdom of God!

Returning to the harvest theme, I recall a conversation in Moscow with Anatoly Rudenko in October 1990. There was widespread concern that 70% of the Russian potato harvest lay ungathered in the ground. I asked Anatoly why so few potatos had been harvested. He explained that under the Communist system, crops were harvested by the enforced mobilisation of large numbers of factory and office workers to the farms for the harvest season. Under an authoritarian regime the system worked; but in the new era of *glasnost* and *perestroika* there were few volunteers! The result? The greater part of the Russian potato harvest rotted in the ground that winter!

If any harvest is not reaped when it is ripe, it will be lost. Is this happening to part of today's spiritual harvest because the churches lack the Scripture tools to bring it in?

November 1998   LOVE

In mid-October I participated in an inspiring service of thanksgiving in London for the life and witness of the Rev A Morgan Derham. Morgan served as UBS Information Officer from 1968 until 1972 when the information officer's position was moved from London to Stuttgart.

Morgan died suddenly last August aged 83. His working life was varied and he saw service with a range of Christian agencies including the Evangelical Alliance (he was partly instrumental in the formation of TEAR Fund which is today a large relief and development agency working in many countries) and the Leprosy Mission as well as the United Bible Societies. His most consistent association over the years was with Scripture Union. Under SU auspices he organised sailing holidays for young people, and right up to his death he remained a popular contributor to SU's *Encounter with God* daily Bible reading notes.

In the thanksgiving sermon, Bishop Gavin Reid underlined, with eloquence and power, Morgan's deep conviction and commitment to the importance of communicating the Bible to children. The bishop challenged the people present to recover this ministry to children and to escape from the `adults only' mentality which characterises so many church services and meetings.

Near the beginning of his ministry Morgan wrote several Christian novels for young people. I still remember the exciting `read' one of these gave me in my early teenage years. It was set in the Norfolk Broads in Eastern England - where Morgan organised his holiday cruises. The book created in me an indelible memory of the unique atmosphere of that attractive network of lakes and waterways.

At the service copies of Morgan's book *Encounter with God in 1 Corinthians* were on sale. I obtained a copy and turned to his commentary on chapter 13: `Love, the Master Key'. On reading and re-reading both chapter and commentary, I was left with two thoughts which I find to be very relevant to us at this point of time in the history of our UBS fellowship as we think about who we are and how we do things. They are two simple, yet very profound thoughts on the importance of demonstrating self-giving Christ-like love in our corporate life.

Love validates

First, love validates all our other gifts and skills. However spectacular or appreciated these may be, they cannot compensate for lack of real caring in our relationships. The spectacular gifts recorded in 1 Corinthians are prophecy and tongues. Perhaps publishing and translation are the Bible Society equivalents! With this contextualisation in mind the following quotation from Morgan is challenging:

> It is not whether we declare the mind of God in prophecy, but whether we communicate the meaning of the love of Christ. It is not whether we move mountains of granite by our faith, but whether we move mountains of suffering by selfless compassion.

Love perpetuates

Second, love perpetuates. 'Love never ends', says Paul in verse 8. 'The only thing we shall carry from this passing world', comments Morgan, 'will be love, Christ-like love (1 Cor 13.7). Prophecies, tongues, healing, words of knowledge - all the exciting paraphernalia of our earthly spirituality - will be finished.'

What a sobering thought this is! What each of us - and each Bible Society - will take with us into the new age to come, will not be our publications, our translation projects, our committees, or our strategy plans. Only love! The love for the Lord and for people which motivates us to do these things! Following the Mississauga Assembly one of our priorities is to encourage every Bible Society to be fully functioning. I wonder, do we sufficiently realise that the most vital Bible Society function of all is to demonstrate the love of Christ in all we do?

Let me finish with one more quotation from Morgan Derham's commentary!

> Today, around the world, in refugee camps, in remote hospitals, in leprosy centres, in orphanages, in favelas, in famine-stricken villages, this love is still being 'poured out' in practical caring by the servants of Jesus. Unlike the popular media, they do not quickly lose interest and move on to some other sensation.

May each of us have love in all we do for the Bible cause and be beautiful in God's sight as well as doing something beautiful for him!

December 1998   FAMILY TREES

During Advent Bible Societies are busy promoting selections containing the nativity story. In many countries the churches use these publications as a key resource to communicate the Christmas message of peace to all people. Undoubtedly Christmas - whether it comes this month for Catholics and Protestants - or next month for the Orthodox Churches - presents Bible Societies with a great opportunity to publish the Good News that God loves the world.

Every Advent and Christmas selection I have seen focuses on the narrative passages in Matthew and Luke, with perhaps some prophetic Old Testament texts and explanatory passages from John's gospel or Paul's epistles.

While the accounts in Matthew and Luke focus on different episodes of the nativity story, one element is found in both: the family tree of Jesus! Yet this component seldom, if ever, appears in our selections!

This is not surprising. Genealogies are not very good `sound bites'! Yet in many cultures ancestry is very important. In fact, the family trees in Matthew 1.2-16 and Luke 3.23-38 contain much which challenges those of us who have been brought up in Western culture. The key is to recognise that the two lineages are not identical. Matthew's works forwards, Luke's backwards. Matthew follows the family line back to Abraham; Luke traces it back to Adam.

Careful study of these two genealogical trees reveals that they implicitly contain the message of Christmas: `Peace on earth to everyone who pleases God!' For both lists of ancestors anticipate Jesus as the one who breaks down the barriers which divide the human race.

Male and Female

The ancient world (and sometimes the modern too!) built barriers between men and women. Sexism was rampant. In his morning prayer, the pious Jewish male thanked God that he had not been made a Gentile, a slave or a woman! In ancient Greek culture women lived a life of utter seclusion with nothing to do apart from household tasks.

Yet Luke highlights a *maternal* family tree, and Matthew selects five women in his ancestral summary. Surely the anticipation of Jesus affording a special place to women!

Black and White

Racism as well as sexism was rampant in the time of the gospels. Anti-Semitism was fashionable and, in return, Jews called the Gentiles `dogs'. `Ethnic cleansing' was not unknown. Although Jesus was a Jew, he would not have been considered ethnically pure because one of his ancestors - Bathsheba - had married a Hittite. Two - Tamar and Rahab - were Canaanites, while one - Ruth - was from Moab.

Again, the genealogies provide a foretaste of Jesus welcoming gentiles into the Kingdom of God.

Sacred and Secular

There is a power play evident in the gospels between the sacred and secular authorities: the Jewish Sanhedrin and the Roman Procurator. Similar tensions are found today in countries that give a special place to one of the great religions.

Intriguingly, the existence of two family trees raises the hope that the person in whom they culminate would break down rigid divisions between the sacred and the secular. While Matthew's tree focuses on the Jews - on Abraham (the prototype believer) and on David (the prototype messiah), Luke's goes back to Adam, embracing the entire human race.

Taken together, they invite us to anticipate that the baby whose birth they announce would be both Head of the church and Lord of the world.

Global and National

First-century Galilee was a hotbed of Jewish nationalism. At least one of Jesus' disciples was a Zealot. So many of Jesus' compatriots believed that they were the only chosen people. They believed other nations were created merely `to stoke the fires of hell'! The world's only hope was to convert to Judaism by becoming God fearers and proselytes.

Again, the existence of two family trees - one national and the other global - anticipates the way in which Jesus affirmed both national and global dimensions. He was true to his national and spiritual heritage and, at the same time, announced God's love for the world. Again, Jesus holds the key to enable us in today's world to respond creatively to the competing trends of economic globalisation and ethnic nationalism.

The genealogies of Jesus are no dead letter. They are as much about today as yesterday. Surely they are a word from the Lord for our Bible Society family! For they:

> - challenge our leadership teams to demonstrate that in Christ there is neither male nor female

> - demand that our corporate UBS structures accord equal recognition to all races in accordance with their gifting

- invite us to exhibit the spirit of Jesus in combining our spiritual mission and institutional existence

- challenge us to find creative ways for the national and the global to interact in our sense of UBS identity.

And to finish, one more thought from the genealogies! By anticipating the kind of person Jesus was to become as well as announcing his arrival, they remind us that Christmas is an opportunity to reflect Christ's lifestyle as well as celebrate his birth.

January 1999   CHOOSE WISDOM

A Happy New Year! May 1999 truly be an *Anno Domini* for all of us - a year in which our lives may glorify the Lord and enjoy him - a year in which our Fellowship of Bible Societies may be found serving faithfully at the cutting edge of the Kingdom of God!

In many cultures the beginning of a New Year is a time for making new resolutions, or vows about how we will live our lives. Alas! All too often these resolutions don't survive long! Too quickly we find ourselves touching down in reality and confessing with St Paul: "For even though the desire to do good is in me, I am not able to do it"!

The New Year is also a time of special offers. Here in Reading stores and shops are having special sales promotions in which `bargains' are temporarily on offer. Perhaps this is why I find myself thinking at this time of year of one the greatest offers in history! The offer the Lord made to King Solomon: 'The Lord appeared to him in a dream and asked him, "What would you like me to give you?"' (1 Kings 3.5).

I'm sure many of us - had we been Solomon - would have asked for:
- a long life, or
- lots of money, or
- success!

But Solomon chose none of these! Instead, he opted for *Wisdom*. `So give me the wisdom I need to rule with justice and to know the difference between good and evil.' (1 Kings 3.9)

It's a real challenge to follow Solomon today! The options he turned down - extended life span, accumulated wealth and realised ambition - are powerful, all-absorbing forces in modern society. Yet none of them holds the key to understanding the universe or of truly enjoying life! According to the Old Testament Book of Proverbs, *wisdom* is that key. Again and again, it tells us that it's much more important to be wise than to become a centenarian, a millionaire, or a celebrity.

The Book of Proverbs is a showcase packed with gems of wisdom. It's a multi-purpose map to guide us on life's journey. The abiding relevance of the Proverbs - which comes home to me especially when I read them in the *Good News Bible* or the *Contemporary English Version* - is summed up in 1.2-4:

> Proverbs will teach you wisdom and self-control and how to understand sayings with deep meanings. You will learn what is right and honest and fair. From these, an ordinary person can learn to be smart, and young people can gain knowledge and good sense. (CEV).

What better way to walk into another year than to carry these biblical one-liners in our minds to ponder and to practise! So please allow me to share with you ten proverbs which have recently spoken to me. All are taken from the CEV.

- *Sometimes you can become rich by being generous or poor by being greedy (11.24)*
- *Do all you can for everyone who deserves your help. Don't tell your neighbour to come back tomorrow, if you can help today (3.27,28)*
- *Wicked people bluff their way, but God's people think before they take a step (21.29)*
- *It's better to obey the Lord and have only a little, than to be very rich and terribly confused (15.16)*
- *Caring for the poor is lending to the Lord, and you will be well repaid (19.17)*
- *Losing self-control leaves you as helpless as a city without a wall (25.28)*
- *A friend you can't trust in times of trouble is like having a toothache or a sore foot (25.19)*
- *If you obey the Lord, you will always know the right thing to say (10.32)*
- *Whoever delivers your message can make things better or worse for you (13.17)*
- *Battles are won by listening to advice and making lots of plans (24.6)*

In conclusion, one final gem from Proverbs:

> **Kind words are like honey - they cheer you up and make you feel strong.** *(16.24)*

Let us all help to make the world a better place in 1999!

YEAR TWO

February 1999   HUMAN RIGHTS

The recent launch of *The Prince of Egypt,* a multi-million dollar animated epic film featuring the life of Moses, has brought one of the Bible's greatest stories into the film theatres of the world.

Is this the answer to our prayers for the message of the Bible to be heard in the public square of our global village?

By any standards the film is impressive. The graphics are superb, and the special effects of dust, shadow and light are awe-inducing. The dialogue is arresting and the story line, while elaborating the biblical narrative, is generally faithful to it.

That is not to say that the film would receive a certificate from our UBS translation consultants! At times the story line diverges from the biblical text: Moses as a baby is not reunited with his mother. He is an eloquent speaker in no need of help from Aaron, and he kills the Egyptian accidentally rather than murdering him. And Aaron plays the role of discourager rather than helper.

On the other hand, the claim in the introduction that the film is `true to the essence, values and integrity' of the story is probably valid. The intention of the makers was not to produce Scripture-on-screen, so much as to provide entertainment with a positive message. And the introduction explicitly spells out the producers' view that this positive message is the enormous impact of the exodus on the great faiths of Judaism, Christianity and Islam and, through them, on world history.

In attempting to answer my opening question about whether *The Prince of Egypt* is the answer to our prayers, I am struck by a remarkable coincidence: the appearance of the blockbuster film coincided with the publication of Pope John Paul II's message for the celebration of the World Day of Peace on 1 January 1999. The title of the Pope's message is `Respect for Human Rights: the Secret of True Peace'.

The contrast between the two media could not be greater. The film employs state of the art animation and special effects; its plot is portrayed against vast landscapes and on sumptuous sets; its cast includes big name movie stars. On the other hand, the papal message comes in the form of a closely argued text, printed in single colour within a very ordinary looking cover.

Yet, the close link between the story line of *The Prince* and the message of the Pope is striking. The rights highlighted in the papal message - the right to life, the right to participate, the right to self-fulfilment, the right to work, and the right to peace - are all inherent in the film. And the Pope's declaration that `religious freedom constitutes the very heart of human rights' could have been the punch line of *The Prince of Egypt*!

This coincidence ought not to surprise us. For human rights have scriptural foundations. They stem from the biblical concept of the inherent dignity and worth of the human person created in the image of God. And many biblical narratives - not just Exodus - reflect the long struggle for human rights.

Perhaps as Bible Societies we need to put greater emphasis on this link between the Bible and human rights. I have found the portion published by the American Bible Society to mark the fiftieth anniversary of the Universal Declaration of Human Rights to be particularly helpful. It places each human right side by side with biblical texts which have significantly contributed towards its articulation and adoption.

I find it helpful because it:

- demonstrates the relevance of Scripture to human rights campaigns and programs

- provides an invaluable resource for Bible Societies wishing to design Scripture selections for churches championing human rights

- stimulates us to think strategically of doing more holistic distribution programs.

Now to answer the question: Is *The Prince of Egypt* the answer to our prayers? Well, perhaps not *the* answer! But I believe it is *an* answer - especially if we take advantage of its popularity to recommend to people that they read the Book of Exodus and encourage them from there to begin to discover the wider message of the Word of God.

Let me leave with you this month a short extract from the Pope John Paul II's message in which he urges us to become `heralds of human dignity':

Faith teaches us that every person has been created in the image and likeness of God. Even when man refuses it, the Heavenly Father's love remains steadfast; his is a love without limits. He sent his Son Jesus to redeem every individual, restoring each one's full human dignity. With this in mind, how can we exclude anyone from our care?

The document recognises the threat to the dignity of the human person posed by political ideologies, racial and ethnic myths, and materialistic consumerism.

It denounces recourse to violence in the name of religion, decreasing world educational opportunities, lack of respect for the environment, uncontrolled proliferation of small arms and light weapons.

All human beings, without exception, are equal in dignity. These rights apply to every stage of life and to every political, social, economic and cultural situation. Together they form a single whole, directed unambiguously towards the promotion of every aspect of the good of both the person and society.

The Pope challenges us to see that rights confer responsibilities. He urges all individuals and all sectors of society to work for the creation of a culture of human rights by committing ourselves to safeguard every human right of all our fellow human beings.

March 1999   STORY-TELLING

Story-telling is regaining its popularity today in the western world. This is a good development because it widens the scope of a medium which has proved itself to be effective in communicating the message of Scripture in other cultures where it has held its ground.

The Bible lends itself to story-telling because it is Good News. Good News is much more than good advice, more than a great yarn, more even than sound theology! The Bible is *Good* News primarily because it records the greatest news story in human history - the story of God's personal intervention to save the world. And it is Good *News* because that story of Christ's birth, death and resurrection is today addressing and changing the lives of individuals and communities worldwide!

And yet so often the Bible's message is presented as a series of ideas rather than as a story. We see this again and again in religious tracts. And Bible Societies also sometimes make this mistake, especially when we publish Scripture selections which do little more than string together a series of biblical thoughts without any reference to the narrative sweep of God's mighty deeds from which these thoughts flow.

I believe the time is ripe for us in the Bible Societies to recommit ourselves to promoting the Bible as story. I say this for three reasons.

First, the Bible is essentially narrative or story.

Not only the chronological sweep of the whole, from creation to new creation, including the various events and developments of what has sometimes been called `salvation history', but also the way the large narrative portions interweave so that they, too, have a place in the ongoing story, while these other materials - parables, hymns, prayers, summaries, theological expositions - serve in different ways to enable readers to get hold of the story and to live their way into it.

(Charles Wood)

Second, there is today a new awareness of the role of stories in social interaction.

Some go so far as to claim that the necessity to tell and hear stories is a fundamental need of the human race, second only to the need for nourishment.

We crave nothing less than perfect story; and while we chatter or listen all our lives in a din of craving - jokes, anecdotes, novels, dreams, films, plays, songs, half the worlds of our days - we are satisfied only by the one short tale we feel to be true: *History is the will of a just God who knows us.* (Reynolds Price).

And third, story-telling is becoming popular in cultures which have become dominated by print and electronic communication.

This confirms Andrew Walker's contention that literacy plus electricity are not a satisfying substitute for orality, and illustrates that lo-tech media can reach parts of our personalities which hi-tech media cannot.

However we tell the Story, *telling* it is vitally important. Because it is only as it is told, that the Scriptures can become Good *News*. After all, news is *news* because it makes an impact and exerts an influence. But there can be no impact if the news is kept secret. It is those who hear and believe its Story, who experience its power in their lives, who discover that the Bible is Good *News*.

So, as we have already said, the Bible is both *Good* and *News*. It is *Good* because it makes the announcement: God so loved the world that he gave his only Son so that whoever believes in him might not die but have eternal life. And it is *News* because translating it, reading it, proclaiming it so often enriches the lives of those who receive it, helping to make the world a better place.

The Bible and storytelling fit together like a hand in a glove! Let us, therefore, grasp the growing popularity of story-telling as a great new opportunity to re-tell the Bible Story in a way which will lift the Word of God off the printed page and help it enter and transform the life of individuals and inform the lifestyle of communities!

A final suggestion on story-telling and the Bible. Listen to the hymn *The old, old story*. It could have been written for the Bible Societies!

Tell me the Old, Old Story of unseen things above,
Of Jesus and his glory, of Jesus and his love.
Tell me the Story simply, as to a little child,
For I am weak and weary, and helpless and defiled.
Tell me the Old, Old Story of Jesus and his love!

April 1999   BIBLE ADVOCACY

This month we are perhaps more conscious than usual of living on the other side of Easter. The great annual celebration of our Lord's resurrection is now behind us, but its impact is still fresh in our memory. We feel inspired to pray with St Paul: `All I want is to know Christ and the power that raised him to life' (Philippians 3.10).

Yet there is a sense in which every Sunday is Easter Sunday! For the resurrection of our Lord is pivotal to our faith, our lifestyle and our view of reality.

- `Life is a larger word than Resurrection; but Resurrection is, so to speak, the crucial quality of life' - William Temple

- `Easter is only another name for Christianity' – Andrew Blackwood

Is death the end? is one of today's great questions. And, as Easter has recently reminded us, it's a question which the New Testament tackles head on.

As our generation approaches a new millennium this and other big questions are coming to the surface. Many of the answers on offer in today's media assume either that we are living in a post-Christian world (`Science is the only test of reality'), or that we are moving back into a pre-Christian framework (`This is the age of Aquarius').

This is the modern market place of ideas. This is the market place in which we as Bible Societies are offering the Bible as Good News for all. The challenge we face is how to demonstrate the relevance of the Bible to the questions people are asking today. Moderns tell us it is too old-fashioned, New Agers that it's not ancient enough! This is why for us Bible advocacy is no longer a straightforward option.

How do we serve as advocates of the Bible? Basically there are only two ways: Listening! And living!

The first is to listen to the questions people are asking. In one sense it is easier to hear these questions today than 50 or 100 years ago, because so many of today's questions are raised on the electronic media which increasingly encompass the world. On the other hand, listening must also take place at the grass roots because fears and questions exist which are specific to particular cultures and peoples.

It might help us to understand our role in Bible advocacy if we take a quick look at three of the big issues which are concerning people the world over.

Is anything real?

One of today's big questions is: `Is anything real?' The electronic culture in which many of us live is changing the nature of perceived reality. Marshall McLuhan tells the story of the mother whose response to the admiring comments of her friends about her new baby was: `You should see his photo!' Our world of television, video and virtual reality is confusing the relationship between pictures and things. As a result sometimes images are perceived as objects in the world, the unreal being understood as real!

This confusion about reality has a knock-on effect on the way people find self-fulfilment.

- Many are turning to drugs in search of an alternative reality.

- Celebrities, like Madonna, meticulously create new images of themselves, one after the other.

How can the Bible help people to answer this question?

- It tells us: `In the beginning God created the heavens and the earth' (Genesis 1.1).

- And it goes on to say: `God created humans to be like himself; he made men and women' (Genesis 1.27).

In other words, the Bible declares that God is an external transcendent reality who has created a real world and real people.

Am I free?

Another key issue for today's generation is: `Am I free?' This perennial question has a new urgency today in the light of `the defeat of Genesis by genetics' which is capturing the imagination of many young thinkers and opinion-makers. A form of neo-Darwinism is filling the vacuum created by the collapse of Marxism and is mounting an assault on the freedom of the will. Humans are simply `Survival machines - robot vehicles blindly programmed to preserve the selfish molecules known as genes'. All our actions, thoughts and feelings, all that we believe, imagine, dream, all that we hope for, love and wonder at are pre-programmed by DNA components into our `robot' brains.

The champions of this genetic fatalism are Richard Dawkins of Oxford and E O Wilson of Harvard. Not surprisingly, they dismiss religion and the Bible as pre-scientific superstition. `Faith', says Dawkins, `is one of the world's great evils, comparable to the smallpox virus, but harder to eradicate.' He even claims that those who teach religion to small children are guilty of `child abuse'!

How can the Bible help people to respond to such claims?

- First, it contains the great declaration of Jesus to his followers: `You will know the truth and the truth shall make you free!' (John 8.32)

- Second, the Bible's great missionary apostle declares, `All things were created by God's Son, and everything was made for him. God's Son was before all else, and by him everything is held together.' (Colossians 1.16,17)

- Third, readers of the Letter to the Ephesians – whose first recipients were brought up to believe that their fate, already written in the stars, was unalterable – are assured that God had set them free by the death of Christ. (1.7)

In other words, the Bible's analysis of the human problem focuses on our sins, not on our genes. It tells us that Jesus Christ died and rose again to set us free from ourselves and enable us to live for God and for others.

Why am I here?

Another question often echoed today is `Why am I here?' At the end of the second millennium people are asking what is life all about. The collapse of Marxism has dealt a death blow to idealism. Cross materialism seems to be taking us over.

- Consumerism carries all before it. `I shop, therefore I am' is the creed of the world's affluent urbanites.

- The genetic fatalism of Dawkins and Williams encourages an egoistic approach to life. `I am for me. Everyone else is a potential item on my menu' is the implicit credo of many. The poor, powerless or marginalised are a nuisance!

And yet many people are inwardly dissatisfied and uneasy with such blatant forms of egoism. Is there not, they ask, something higher to live for?

The Bible's message is that there certainly is! Two sayings from Jesus and a single sentence from St Paul are enough to demonstrate this:

- *Jesus*: When asked: 'Which is the greatest commandment?', he replied: 'Love the Lord your God with all your heart, with all your soul, and with all your mind'. This is the greatest and most important commandment. The second most important commandment is like it: 'Love your neighbour as you love yourself.' (Matthew 22.37-39)

- *Jesus*: `I came so that everyone would have life and have it in its fullest' (John 10.10). Jesus offers people real fulfilment!

- *Paul*: 'Whatever you do... do it all for God's glory.' (1Corinthians 10.31)

In other words, the Bible makes clear that human happiness is a by-product, not an end-product. It's a by-product of glorifying God and of serving others!

Is anything real? - Am I really free? - What am I doing here?

The Bible *does* address big issues like these. Because God's Word abides for ever it is always relevant! But simply *saying* this is not enough. Ultimately we become effective advocates of the Bible only by *living* out its message in the everyday world!

And finally, one additional seed-thought on the link between Easter and Bible Society work:

'The Gospels do not explain the Resurrection; the Resurrection explains the Gospels' – John S Whale

May 1999   SOIL TESTING

I remember Russell Self – one of our distinguished distribution consultants of the time – telling the 1980 Chiang Mai World Assembly (or Council as it then was) that Jesus' parable of the Sower is about soil testing as well as seed sowing. He was advocating the use in Scripture publishing of market research, and judging by the increased focus on receptor needs since Chiang Mai, his words did not fall on deaf ears.

Research is also useful in helping to evaluate how effectively the Fellowship follows up the rallying-cries of World Assemblies. The telephone survey conducted at the end of last year on behalf of UBS by a professional marketing research agency sought to do this for the 1996 Mississauga Assembly. The results indicate that, two years on, Bible Societies are continuing to affirm the goals set by Mississauga, but many are struggling to find the resources and help to put these programs into practice.

Based on 150 interviews of national Bible Society Board Chairs and General Secretaries, and conducted in English, Spanish, French and Russian, the survey also revealed strong support for the draft UBS Mission Statement produced by the Structure Review Group (formerly the TTM Task Team) as an expression of our identity and ethos set in the world of the 21st century and celebrating the wealth and diversity of our global Fellowship.

Mission and Service

The section of the Mississauga Document most consistently prioritised by those interviewed was `Serving Together: The Bible Societies and the Churches'. Nine out of ten respondents identified this as an area either extremely relevant or very relevant to their Bible Society's work. Almost one third spontaneously expressed the view that Bible Society-Church relations need strengthening and that Bible Societies should be more responsive to, and aware of, the needs and preferences of the churches.

The second area of the Mississauga statement which received very high prioritisation was `Scriptures for all: Production and distribution, the ongoing challenge'. Effective distribution was spontaneously referred to by more than half of those interviewed, and many Bible Societies see this as *the* core activity.

`In all tongues: Translation, the unfinished task' scored highly, especially in Africa and the Americas, but much less in Europe, Middle East and Asia. The section of the Document entitled `Providing the resources for Scripture needs: Fundraising' also scored very highly, particularly among African Bible Societies.

Good feed-back was also received on the Mississauga goals relating to research, new technology, developing human resources and increasing our sense of global fellowship. A detailed report on the survey is being prepared by Jon Jeffery, our Research Consultant, and will be available to the Fellowship in due course.

Some of you have expressed frustrations that telephone problems and language difficulties prevented you from participating as freely as you would have liked, and others of you are disappointed that you were not called. I apologise for any inconveniences and oversights which occurred and assure you that we are investigating with the research agency all specific complaints received.

However, despite such shortcomings, the survey clearly confirms that mission is a primary concern of Bible Societies! How to reach new and previously unserved audiences? How best to help the churches reach out to those who have lost their faith, to young people, to the dispossessed and to the non-literate are clearly issues which deeply concern many of us.

Another consistent theme, especially in relation of the proposed Mission Statement, is a desire for the UBS World and Regional Service Centers to provide more inspiring, encouraging and envisioning leadership.

The survey provides very helpful guidance for planning the program for the next World Assembly in 2000. For example, it confirms that people find interaction with others in the Fellowship to be creative, but are less than enthusiastic about workshops on subjects with which they are already familiar.

The next World Assembly

The forthcoming Assembly in Midrand, South Africa, in October 2000 is being designed as a working assembly. It will encourage the active and audible participation of all Bible Societies and is expected to take very important decisions about the identity, ethos, structures and strategies with which the Fellowship will move forward into the next century.

Because of this effective participation of all Bible Societies in the preparation for the Assembly will be as important as in the Assembly itself. The same will be true for the follow up to the Assembly after it is over.

The preparation process has already begun. In November and December the telephone survey obtained Bible Society reactions to the draft Mission Statement. Last March Regional Committees provided very helpful comment on a series of options for the shape of a new global Board and possible new regional governance structures. Later this month Bible Societies will be asked to share their initial response to these proposals.

It is intended that this consultative interaction with Bible Society Boards and staff will continue until shortly before Midrand in the hope that when the Assembly *takes* final decisions, these decisions will in effect have been *made* by the whole Fellowship over a period of time and after considerable reflection and prayer. So as we all prepare for the Midrand Assembly the message from UBSEC, the Assembly Task Team and the Structure Review Group is: `Keep talking! We're listening!'

This is the name of the game!

June 1999   SCRIPTURE DISTRIBUTION

This month I want to raise the question: Is Scripture distribution always appropriate?

Surely to ask such a question sounds like Bible Society heresy! But this is the dilemma which the Bible Societies in the Balkan countries of southern Europe have been facing. Do they organise the distribution of Scriptures among Kosovan refugees who have been flooding in large numbers into neighbouring countries? Our UBS reflexes prompt us to say `Yes, of course!' But the answer may not be so clear cut.

Ninety-nine per cent of the refugees are Muslims. They have been forced out of their homes and communities by soldiers from a country with strong Christian traditions. So, how are they going to react if given a piece of their oppressor's Holy Scriptures? How will the Kosovans respond to a message offering forgiveness and demanding repentance? To them, this message must seem to be misdirected, for in this conflict they are the sinned-against, not the sinners. In such a context will not Scripture distribution do more harm than good?

I am sure the Balkan Bible Societies will value the prayers of the whole Fellowship as they struggle with this dilemma. And as a stimulus to our prayers for Kosovo and Kosovans I want this month to think through with you the principles involved.

It seems to me that there are two issues of principle to be resolved.

Indiscriminate or selective?

The first is: Should distribution be indiscriminate or selective?

The Parable of the Sower involves indiscriminate broadcasting of the seed to cover every type of soil in the field. Situations today where this method is particularly appropriate are: Scriptures prepared for radio, television, posters and newspapers.

But the New Testament also gives examples of narrow casting. Think of St Paul's exhortation in Colossians 4.5,6. `Be wise,' he says, `in the way you act towards those who are not believers, making good use of every opportunity you have. Your speech should always be pleasant and interesting, and you should know how to give the right answer to everyone.' (GNB)

According to one of the great English biblical scholars of a century ago, Bishop J B Lightfoot, the point being made by the apostle is that Christian conversation must not only be `opportune as regards the time; it must also be appropriate as regards the person'.

Of course, St Paul has in view the words of Christians rather than the words of Scripture. But the application of what he says regarding the first can legitimately be extended to the second. The message for us is this: our distribution strategies should be sensitive to the needs and circumstances of those who are to receive the Scriptures. To distribute Scriptures indiscriminately to people who are traumatised by what they regard as `Christian' oppression, will probably alienate rather than reconcile the recipients.

Pietistic or holistic?

The second issue is: Can Scripture distribution ever be detached from the other activities of Christian mission?

Early in his ministry Jesus announced his `Nazareth Manifesto' (Luke 4.16-30), promising to integrate redemption and relief. And he certainly did this over the following three years as he moved from place to place, healing the sick, defending the poor, and touching the lepers, as well as preaching the good news of the kingdom of God.

This is why a purely pietistic strategy among the Kosovans would be inappropriate. It is as Christian workers from churches and aid agencies help the refugees in practical ways, getting to know them, becoming their friends and demonstrating God's love, that the Christians will re-gain integrity in the eyes of the refugees. Once that happens, the development of personal acquaintance and friendship will enable the Scriptures to be given with honour and received with dignity.

In a chapter entitled `Holistic mission in theological perspective', in the MARC book called *Serving with the Poor in Latin America*, C Rene Padilla of Argentina, underlines that the message of the gospel is inseparable from the messenger's life. `Proclaiming the gospel is not an activity but a lifestyle articulated by words and action', says the author.

So, to return to the question with which we began: Is Scripture distribution always appropriate? Surely the answer is `Yes, but...'. The `but' highlights the kind of qualifications we've just noted. Motivation and methodology are important. For any program of Scripture distribution which is insensitive to the feelings of recipients or detached from the broader mission of the church is surely less than Christian. But when distribution programs respond to felt needs and are part of a wider ministry of caring, then the Scriptures are often warmly received and appreciated.

The great watchword of the well-known American leadership guru, Stephen Covey, is to make our lives principle-centred. In his best-seller, 'The 7 Habits of Highly Effective People', he identifies four fundamental life support factors on which all of us depend. These are: security, guidance, wisdom and power.

· **Security** is our emotional anchorage which provides our basic personal strength.

· **Guidance** is our source of direction in life, that which governs our decision-making and our doing.

· **Wisdom** is our perspective on life, which determines how we view the world.

· **Power** is the vital energy to act and accomplish.

Covey suggests that life is like a wheel which has these four factors as its spokes. As the spokes unite axle and rim, so these factors hold our lives together. Security, guidance, wisdom and power are vital features in the personalities of people who find life fulfilling.

But spokes without an axle have no strength! So the quality of the security, guidance, wisdom and power we enjoy depends on what we put at the centre of our lives! Covey's argument is that principles make strong axles, and that other things make weak axles.

He identifies a series of alternative centres around which many build their lives – self, work, money, spouse, family, possessions, pleasure, friend/enemy and even church. Although some of these are attractive and commendable, they make faulty axles. Focusing singularly on any one of these and making our lives revolve around it, will rob us of the sense of fulfillment and enjoyment for which we have been created and redeemed.

Don't forget that our life support factors – the spokes of the wheel – when they are well secured to the axle, will make our lives more authentic as well as more fulfilling! This is particularly important today when so many people are searching for authentic spirituality.

The Word at the centre

The thought I want to leave with you this month is on the importance of making God's Word the centre of our lives. The seductive power of the alternative axles is strong, and we need constantly to relocate the Word at the centre of our lives. To do this effectively it is helpful to remember that God has given us his Word in two forms.

First, we have his Word in the form of his incarnate Son. The Lord Jesus Christ is the Word *par excellence* (John 1.1-14). We are called to acknowledge his Lordship day by day as we discover and re-discover in him our security (John 10.28), guidance (John 8.12), wisdom (1 Corinthians 1.24) and power (1 Corinthians 1.24).

The second form of God's Word is in the Holy Scriptures which have been given as a lamp to give light wherever we walk. As we spend time reading, hearing and meditating on the Bible, God's Word becomes our means of security (Psalm 119.114), guidance (Psalm 119.46), wisdom (Psalm 19.7) and power (Psalm 119.46).

As we honour Jesus as Lord by obeying what he says to us in and through the Holy Scriptures, our lives will indeed be principle-centred!

August 1999   REDWOODS

'The Avenue of the Giants' is a famous scenic highway through 51,222 acres of giant redwood groves in Northern California. It is 31 miles (almost 50 kms) long and winds its way through Humboldt Redwoods State Park, which is, perhaps, the most outstanding display of these giant trees in the world.

Dolina, my wife, and I recently visited this beautiful part of California. As we walked in the cool shade of these magnificent giants of the forest towering above us, we became very conscious of the grandeur of God's creation, and the wonder and beauty of trees.

This experience, together with the Bible's use of the tree as symbol (Genesis 2 and 3; Revelation 22) and parable (Psalm 1, Mark 4.30-32, etc.) has prompted me to consider that these giant redwoods have some lessons for us today. Allow me to share three reflections which relate to our work in the UBS.

Potentiality

The Sequoia Redwoods are the largest living things in the world – larger even than the mighty whale, and perhaps larger than any plant or animal that ever lived on earth. A giant Sequoia can weigh as much as 6 million pounds – the weight of 800 buses! - and contain sufficient wood to construct 40 timber homes of 5 rooms each!

And yet these enormous redwoods can grow from a seed that weighs less than a small feather – 1/8000th of an ounce! In this sense a redwood seed, no less than the mustard seed of Jesus' parable, illustrates that sometimes the Kingdom of God can have very humble beginnings (Mark 4.30-32). It also reminds us that when we share a Scripture selection with someone else, under God, the results can be very much greater than we imagine at the time!

Community

The Coast Redwoods are the tallest trees in the world, soaring at times to the height of a 35-story building! They are nicknamed `God's flagpoles' because they grow so straight. One of the secrets of their straightness is that they grow together in groves, in marked contrast with the single examples of some other tree species on the northern Californian coast which are bushy through lack of company and bent over by the prevailing wind.

The tree giants form not only a community in themselves; they are the main feature of a wider complex community of plants and animals, many of which depend on each other for survival. In fact both the Coast Redwoods and the Sequoia Redwoods are known as `climax communities' because the trees live in harmony with the surrounding plants and animals so that no new species will naturally come along and replace them.

Is not this is a picture of our UBS fellowship – and, indeed, any Christian fellowship? We are called to be a community of harmony, consensus (which is not to be confused with unanimity!), sharing, inter-dependence – a community in which every member feels `safe' and fully accepted by the others.

Recovery

When a Coast Redwood falls or is cut down, sprouts shoot up from the stump and from the roots. Some of these sprouts in time grow into giant Redwoods. Since the new tree grows from the same root system as the old, it is essentially the same tree. In some cases, a Coast Redwood might have been reborn many times over the millennia.

Here we find an echo with another biblical parable. Isaiah offers hope to defeated Israel – see Isaiah 6.13 and 11.1. I like the GNB rendering of 6.13: `The stump represents a new beginning for God's people'.

As with ancient Israel, so also with us today – in our personal lives, in our family life, in our churches and, even in our Bible Societies – disaster may strike. But it need not be the end! The stump of God's work in us and of his purpose through us offers us a new beginning. Thank God that his gospel - our good news - is a message of redemption, of restoration, of recovery!

Finally, let us carry with us in our minds the beautiful lines of Joyce Kilmer as an *aide memoire* to the parable of the Redwoods:

> I think that I shall never see
> A poem lovely as a tree.
> Poems are made by fools like me,
> But only God can make a tree.

Sept 1999   NEHUSHTAN

This month I want to share with you some reflections on Nehushtan.

Nehushtan? A distant country? Rock band? New drug?

No, it's none of these! It's the copper serpent Moses lifted up near the Gulf of Aqaba when large numbers of Israelites were dying from poisonous snake bites in the desert . The Book of Numbers 21.4-9 vividly describes the event.

The copper snake was a symbol, not a saviour, according to ancient Jewish tradition (see *The Wisdom of Solomon* 16.6,7).

Not surprisingly, perhaps, over succeeding centuries the copper snake came to be revered for its own sake, and by the time of King Hezekiah (about 700 BC), the people were burning incense in its honour (2 Kings 18.4). The icon had become an idol!

Hezekiah was a reforming king and did not hesitate to act. He took the revered national emblem and dramatically broke it in pieces! It may have been he who gave it the name *Nehushtan* which means `a piece of copper', to underline that the bronze serpent was no more than that.

Does the action of the iconoclast king of Judah have any lessons for today? Over two and a half millennia separate us from him. He was king of a tiny buffer state in the ancient world within which he exerted enormous influence. By contrast we are increasingly powerless citizens of a globalised economic community.

The parallels between Hezekiah and ourselves are not obvious. And yet, there is a link between us. For in our secularised modern world, old icons are becoming new idolatries. And these subtle new idolatries are every bit as dangerous as the copper serpent had become in Jerusalem twenty-seven hundred years ago. They have insinuated themselves into the thinking of churches and para-church bodies like UBS, threatening to rob us of our sense of dependence on God.

So, what are these latter day Nehustans? What are these icons-cum-idols which threaten us from within?

Allow me to suggest three. Like the bronze serpent, all three have fulfilled a God-given role which has contributed significantly to our development as a global Fellowship. But like Nehushtan, they have developed a power of their own and threaten to become rivals to God!

Change

One candidate for the Nehushtan classification is *Change*.

This is surprising, because, unlike the ancient Greek philosophers, Christians are positive about change. The Bible is a story of change and the Good News is a powerful agent of change. The Word of God encourages us to grasp change as an opportunity to grow, to develop, to move forward. Some of the key developments in the history of Christian mission came about because Christians decided to do things differently. And in our fast moving world of today, the prizes go to those churches and agencies which are sufficiently flexible in their structure to respond quickly to new needs and opportunities.

But, like the copper serpent, change can become an end rather than a means. Perhaps this is especially a temptation of innovative organisations which want to be at the cutting edge of progress. Change converts into an idol when it is initiated for its own sake and diverts us from our mission.

Eugene Peterson perceptively contrasts change with growth. Speaking of western society he says:

> Our culture is filled with change; it's poor in growth. New things, models, developments, opportunities are announced, breathlessly, every hour. But instead of becoming ingredients in a long and wise growth, they simply replace. The previous is discarded and the immediate stuck in, until, bored by the novelty, we run after the next fad. Men and women drawn always to the new never grow up. God's way is growth, not change. (*The Message of David*, p. 136).

That is why change *per se* is not virtuous. By itself it does not produce growth.

And it can even become vicious and destabilise an organisation when it produces replacement without development

Recognising the limitations of change helps us to demythologise it. After all, that's what Hezekiah did to Nehushtan!

Management

Another of today's candidates for idol status is *Management*.

Again, at first sight this comes as surprise. St Paul compares Christian leaders to `stewards' who were managers of large first century households. Modern management has become one of the hallmarks of Christian enterprise in the late 20th century. And there is no doubt that missions have benefited enormously as a result. In fact, it can be convincingly argued that the marrying of management practice to mission strategy in the last 25 years has been used by God to accelerate church growth in many countries on a scale unprecedented in the entire Christian era.

But now there are signs that the pendulum may have swung too far. Samuel Escobar has called for the abandonment of a type of `managerial missiology' which leaves little if any room for the Holy Spirit. There is a new appreciation of the limitations of the market analogy to the task of the churches. After all, the Good News is not Coca Cola!

In addition, management can actually be detrimental if it replaces, rather than enhances, leadership in the churches. Management is methodical and technical; leadership is visionary and strategic. Unless it is twinned with leadership, management depersonalises even Christian institutions. In a documentary programme shown on the UK's Channel 4 last month a former management consultant confessed:

> We've driven the life out of people, driven the passion out of people, and driven the passion out of products.

The icon has become an idol!

IT

My third candidate for the Nehushtan wooden spoon is *IT*!

Today Information Technology is one of the icons of progressive Christian organisations. Any mission agency without computers, databases, email and Web site is regarded as living in the dark ages!

Again, this identification of IT with Nehushtan at first seems unfair and reactionary. For there is no doubt that the harnessing of IT is helping churches and missions to achieve more in shorter periods of time. And the need in this information age for Christian enterprises to invest in the ongoing communications revolution is self-evident.

But if the product of IT remains as no more than information, then this third icon of contemporary mission endeavor needs to be challenged! What use is information if we lack the time to absorb it, reflect upon it and interpret it? When information parades as knowledge has it not become an idol?

In the 1995 London Lectures on Contemporary Christianity, organised by Julia Bicknell, Senior Broadcast Journalist, BBC News and Current Affairs, one of the lecturers, Alan Rogers, made this telling observation:

> Bear in mind that there is a difference between acquiring information and being educated. Information and knowledge are not the same. One might say that knowledge is 'information with an attitude', that knowledge is partly built up of information that has been processed and shaped and framed to be educational. Roaming the Internet picking up random information is not educational. Education needs structure and meaning. (*The Word on the Box*, ed. David Porter, p.75)

As Christians we are committed to communicating the Good News educationally, for the Lord commands us 'to make disciples'. For this reason we can never be satisfied with any communication strategy which focuses only on information. Information requires to be processed so that it leads to knowledge, and knowledge requires to be evaluated in the light of Scripture and Christian tradition and experience so that it leads to wisdom. And all three – information, knowledge and wisdom – require to be communicated throughout the organisation.

This is why IT as such is only part of the answer to the challenge of communication today.

A Hezekiah strategy

So, how are we to prevent these icons becoming idols? Hezekiah points us to a solution. When the bronze snake became an idol he declared it to be Nehushtan - only a piece of copper! And he demonstrated the truth of his declaration by breaking the symbol in pieces.

Of course, in one sense Hezekiah's strategy was specific to him and the challenge he faced. It would be unwise for us to ban change, do away with management or dismantle IT! But we do well to demythologise them and break their spell! They have a vital role in their own place, as the bronze snake had in the desert. But that role is to serve God's church, not to mesmerise it!

And finally…

All has not yet been said about the bronze serpent! Its significance as an icon is highlighted in the Gospel of John 3.14. There we are told that it points away from itself to the crucifixion and exaltation of the Son of Man. This Johannine footnote challenges us as we move towards the 21ˢᵗ century to ensure that our UBS icons of change, management and IT are used, not only to serve the mission of our Fellowship, but also in such ways that they will reflect Jesus' denial of himself for the sake of others, and point to his glory as the Lord of eternal life.

Oct 1999   CELEBRITY

Newspapers, magazines, radio and television stations world wide are urging us to vote for our `Person' of the Century, or even of the Millennium'. Some media have already announced their findings, and there is a certain predicability about it all. The age-old assumption that the `famous' are the eminently successful still holds. Maybe the only difference in the late 20ᵗʰ century is that the successful must also have a pleasing personality!

What is real fame? The Bible points to the answer! It tells us that the real status of anyone is determined by what he or she is before God. Several of Jesus' parables make this point. So also do the historical books of the Old Testament. There the kings of ancient Israel and Judah are evaluated, not by their political or military achievements, but by whether they `obeyed the Lord' or `disobeyed the Lord' (CEV). The NRSV is more literal: the rulers either `did what was right in the sight of the Lord' or `did what was evil in the sight of the Lord'.

Headline or Footnote?

People appraisal from a divine viewpont was as unusual in the days of the Old Testament kings as it is in ours. Take the case of Omri, king of the northern kingdom of Israel from BC 885 to 874. The writer of Kings dismisses him in six terse verses (1Kings 16.23-28) – little more than an extended footnote! But his contemporaries gave Omri headlines!

> - The Moabite Stone – a monument dating from about BC 830, commemorating the victories of Mesha, king of Moab over Israel (2 Kings 3.4) – acknowledges that Omri had earlier conquered Moab.

- For a hundred and fifty years after Omri - long after his dynasty had been overthrown - the annals of the Assyrian kings consistently refer to Israel as `the land of the house of Omri'.

- Omri created Samaria as the new capital of Israel with such massive fortifications that it held off the Assyrian army – at the time the most powerful in the world– for three years before finally having to surrender in BC 721.

- Omri laid the foundation for the economic expansion of the northern kingdom which was to reach `boom' proportions, first in the reign of his son Ahab (BC 874-852) and, again, during the long reign of Jeroboam II (BC 793-753). Samaria's strategic position controlling the main trade routes through the Esdraelon plain enabled Omri and his successors to collect lucrative tolls from passing caravans.

Truth and Justice

If these were Omri's achievements, why does he fare so unfavourably in the Bible? The writer of Kings identifies two fatal flaws.

The first was his cavalier attitude to *truth*. Omri was a born opportunist. He discovered that idolatry could serve his political ambition, so he used it.!

He gave his strong support to the cult focused on calf-images of gold in Bethel and Dan set up by Jeroboam I, designed to ensure Israel's religious independence from Judah and the Jerusalem temple. Omri also gave his patronage to Baal worship through the arranged marriage of his son Ahab to Jezebel, daughter of Ethbaal, the priest-king of Tyre and Sidon. An arrangement which worked wonders for Israelite trade!

Omri provides us with a fascinating case study illustrating St Paul's famous analysis that idolatry (a) `suppresses' (NRSV) truth, and (b) exchanges the truth for a lie (Romans 1.18,25).

Omri's second flaw was his failure to uphold *justice*. His economic miracle was built on the backs of the poor. The poor were forced to borrow from the rich at exorbitant interest rates and had to mortgage their land, as well as themselves and their children, in security (see 2 Kings 4.1). The forthright denunciation of such injustice by Elijah and Elisha at the beginning, and by Amos and Hosea at the end, of Israel's `golden age' is reason enough to understand why the writer of Kings did not see greatness in the house of Omri.

But I can hear someone asking: 'What does Omri's low rating in 2 Kings have to do with the UBS?' The answer is 'Everything'. Because we also will ultimately be judged from the perspective of `the eyes of the Lord'. The key questions we have to ask ourselves are these:

- *Are we obeying the mandate the Lord has given us?* This was the all-important measure against which Omri and his fellow kings were judged.

- *Do we do so in ways which honour him?* Truth and justice are as important to our Bible Societies' corporate ethos as they were to the social vision of the Old Testament

The effectiveness of our Bible Societies and the UBS will be measured against this biblical template, just as surely as were the ancient kingdoms of Israel and Judah!

Our contemporaries may erect monuments to commemorate what we do. But someone has said a footprint is a more healthy spiritual indicator than a monument! For, while a monument signifies that we've been there, a footprint indicates that we've moved on! Which will our Bible Society leave in the 20th century?

The Omri syndrome can overcome us as individuals as much as it can affect our Bible Societies and churches! When affluence and success become our great priorities they slowly rob us of our concern for people. Like Naboth in Ahab's eyes, others become objects to be used , not people to be respected and served. The way of Jesus is to follow truth, justice and love - before God and neighbour.

Nov 1999   REACHING CHILDREN

It is now over 5 years since Bryant Myers of World Vision International, writing in the *International Bulletin of Missionary Research*, challenged churches and mission agencies to re-think their strategies for reaching the growing number of the world's children and youth. His article entitled *State of the World's Children: Critical Challenge to Christian Mission* argued forcefully that `understanding the situation of children and youth in the world is a significant blind spot in Christian mission'.

Basic Facts

Dr Myers highlighted the following basic facts:

- One third of the world's population is under the age of 15, and 85% of these children and youth live in the Two-Thirds World.

- The great majority of people make life-shaping decisions before they reach the age of 20.

- 80% of the world's young people are growing up in non-Christian settings or non-Christian homes.

In addition, many children are vulnerable and being shamelessly exploited:

- 100 million children – 18 percent of all children under 15 – live or work on city streets.

- Between 90 million and 145 million children under the age of 15 are exploited as child labourers.

- As many as 10 million children are caught up in the sex industry: in child prostitution, sex tourism and pornography.

Bryant Myer's contention is that most of today's strategies to reach the world with the Good News of Jesus Christ have a strong adult bias and are not relevant to children. This helps to explain the sad fact that the great majority of the world's children and young people have not yet heard the Good News or discovered the Kingdom of God!

Biblical Focus

This negative bias against children is not new. We find it in the harsh early First century Judaism which Jesus had to confront. The chief priests and teachers of the Law became angry when children dared to shout in the temple, `Praise to David's Son!' (Matthew 21.15). And the disciples scolded the people who brought children to Jesus that he might bless them (Matthew 21.13; Mark 10.13; Luke 18.15). Official religion was for adults and for men; women and children didn't count! We have literal confirmation of this in the calculation of numbers – following the convention of the time – at the feeding of the 5,000 and of the 4,000 (`not counting women and children' (Matthew 14.21; 15.38)).

But Jesus refused to accept this downgrading of people whom he fully accepted as citizens of the Kingdom of God. He was `angry' when he discovered his disciples were turning away the children (Mark 10.14). He roundly rebuked the Twelve for failing to understand that his loving purposes embraced children as much as adults.

From Jesus' interaction with his disciples on this and other occasions, we learn three things about his attitude to children.

First, Jesus sees children as *important*.

- The Kingdom of God belongs to them (Mark 10.14).

- Jesus blesses children. He was asked simply to touch them, but he went further. He took them in his arms (Mark 10.16). He welcomed them with open arms!

- Jesus taught that serving a child is the greatest human service anyone can offer. If we welcome a child in Christ's name, we in effect welcome Christ and the Father who sent him (Matthew 18.1-5; Mark 9.33-37; Luke 9.46-48).

Jesus would never say: `It's only a child.'

Second, Jesus sees children as *participant*.

For Jesus, children are participants rather than spectators in religion. He regarded the children as participating in the action of the adults (presumably parents) carried out on the children's behalf. The parents brought the children. But Jesus saw the children, not as passengers, but as participants. He said: `Let the *children* come to me…' So we are not surprised when on another occasion he defended the children shouting in the temple (Matthew 21.16). Clearly Jesus wants children to be seen and heard in church!

Third, Jesus sees children as *significant*.

Children are special signs from God to us. For they remind us of the helplessness and humility we must have to enter the Kingdom of God (Matthew 18.3,4). Unless we receive the Kingdom of God like a child we will never enter it (Mark 10.15; Luke 18.17). George Macdonald, the nineteenth century Scottish writer said that none of us can be a follower of Jesus if children are afraid to play at our door!

Our Response

The challenge we face in the Bible Societies is to undertake what John Stott describes as `double listening'. To listen afresh to what Jesus says about children, and at the same time, to listen to what the Holy Spirit is saying to us through what is happening to children in today's world. Such double listening will enable us to develop strategies which will communicate God's Word effectively to the children of the Third Millennium.

Past World Assemblies have exhorted Bible Societies to produce more Scriptures for children. And some have responded creatively, developing exciting biblical programs for children. But sadly there are others where children's

Scriptures are a low priority. So perhaps the time is now ripe to develop a new comprehensive program which will enable us to sustain a high priority for children in the range of Scriptures funded through the World Service Program.

This will mean taking seriously the felt needs of the 8 in every 10 young people who are outside the churches, and will also mean seeking to relate the Word of God to their aspirations. It will also require avoiding patronising approaches which provide programs for children rather than involving them as key participants with opportunity to help shape the programs.

Finally, the Psalmist tells us that children are a gift from the Lord – a real blessing; they are like arrows in a soldier's hand (Psalm 127.3,4). Is not the key to enabling the Word of God speak to everyone in the 21st century, to reach the children of today and help them become the arrows of tomorrow's Church!

Dec 1999   **ADVENT**

In this season of Advent, Christians the world over are joyfully celebrating one of the two unique events in the history of salvation – the birth of Jesus in Bethlehem. How important it is that we create space amid the consumerism and the entertainment of the modern Christmas to thank God for his unspeakable gift!

Although the Bible Society movement from its inception has studiously tried to avoid `doctrinal note and comment,' it has always assumed that the doctrine of the incarnation is the basis of all that Bible Societies do! The translation of the Holy Scriptures into vernacular languages is essentially incarnational. If the Living Word became incarnate, then it follows that the written Word must also become incarnate in the language and culture of every people. God sent Jesus to us in a form we can perceive and understand, in order that Jesus, in turn, might send us to others with the Good News in a form that they can perceive and understand.

In fact, the incarnation is the model for our mission, identity and ethos! If this is so, then the run up to Christmas is the season for some serious reflection by us, as to how far our corporate UBS culture reflects the first Christmas.

The incarnation is summed up in the New Testament phrase: `God sent his Son'. There are in particular three occurrences of this phrase which contain important lessons for all engaged in serving the Bible cause. These three instances are: 1 John 4.9; Galatians 4.4; and Hebrews 1.1. All three come from different New Testament authors, and each one gives a distinct reason *why* God sent his Son.

To Demonstrate

In 1 John we read that God sent his Son to demonstrate his love.

> **God's love was revealed among us in this way: God sent his only Son into the world so that we might live through him.**
>
> **(1 John 4.9, NRSV)**

`God is love' (1 John 4.8) is one of the great assertions of the New Testament. Prior to making this great statement, John had underlined the vital importance of affirming the flesh-and-blood reality of Jesus Christ (1 John 4.2). And immediately after making it, he pointed to the supreme manifestation of God's love in sending his Son `to be the sacrifice by which our sins are forgiven' (1 John 4.10, CEV). In reality, both the birth and the death of Jesus are demonstrations of God's love. Christmas and Easter are inextricably linked!

But John's concern is that this divine love should be exhibited in the inter-personal relationships of the Christian community. `My dear friends, we must love each other. Love comes from God, and when we love each other, it shows that we have been given new life' (1 John 4.7, CEV).

Is not this as much a challenge to us in the Bible Society family today as it was for the original readers of 1 John? For, It challenges the way we handle our:

- Work ethic
- Management style
- Cross-cultural communication
- Governance processes

and much more besides. It challenges us to esteem one another highly, to believe the best rather than the worst, to be able to express and hear an opposing opinion without losing friends, to help one another to realise a greater potential in their life and in work.

There is a sense in which Christmas should be celebrated in the corporate culture of our Bible Societies and of the UBS, not only in December or January, but in all the other months as well!

To Liberate

St Paul tells us that God sent his Son to set his children free:

50

But when the time was right, God sent his Son, and a woman gave birth to him. His Son obeyed the Law, so he could set us free from the Law, and we could become God's children. (Galatians 4.4f, CEV)

Paul's concern when he wrote these words was for the faith of the Galatian Christians to mature so that they would enter into the full rights of the children of God. If, indeed, these rights are conferred on believers as the direct result of God's act in sending his Son, ought we not to celebrate that act as the apostle did? The fact that the UBS family embraces a wide range of Christian spirituality is no excuse for disavowing our responsibilities to pray and work for the spiritual growth of all our colleagues in the Bible cause! We are to build up one another in the body of Christ until `all of us come to the unity of the faith and of the knowledge of the Son of God, to maturity, the the measure of the full stature of Christ' (Ephesians 4.13)

At the first Christmas the Son of God became like us in order that we might become like him! This Christmas, therefore, let us pray that we might help this ultimate purpose of the incarnation to be advanced in one another!

To Communicate

According to the writer to the Hebrews, God sent his Son to bring his message to us.

Long ago in many ways and at many times God's prophets spoke his message to our ancestors. But now at last, God sent his Son to bring his message to us (Hebrews 1.1f, CEV)

It follows that Christmas is for sharing! Not simply in exchanging presents, but in telling the Good News. In most countries, churches attract bumper congregations at Christmas services – in fact, many more people than at any other time. Christmas provides most churches with their greatest opportunity of the year! And Bible Societies are delighted to help them take fuller advantage of the opportunity by providing attractive Scripture selections containing the Nativity texts.

I sometimes wonder if we sufficiently appreciate the global significance of Christmas for the UBS. It is the time when our selections simultaneously impact millions of people! As this year again we assist the churches to broadcast the Good Seed globally, ought we not to pray more than we do for Bible Societies' Christmas distribution programs? For if these Christmas selections are to impact many lives and create an appetite in recipients to discover more

51

of God's Word, then the Holy Spirit must bring the printed text to life. And the Lord himself tells us that God gives his Spirit to those who ask – see Luke 11.13.

I am writing these words during a visit to Kenya. This letter has taken more than one sitting to finish, and I am glad that this has been so. Because between beginning and ending it, Dr G A Mikre-Sellassie, one of our African UBS Translation Consultants, took me to the town of Machakos to visit the three translators working on the Kikamba common language translation of the New Testament. It was a great pleasure to meet Father Urbanus Kioko (Catholic), Revd Michael Ndonye (Anglican) and Pastor Julius Wambua (African Inland Church).

I found it absolutely fascinating to listen in for a morning as they grappled with the challenges of communicating the Letter of James in words and phrases which their fellow Kambas will recognise and understand as their own language. The visit to Machakos was a pointer to Christmas! For it gave me the privilege of witnessing my four African brothers sending God's Word into the world of the Kamba people, continuing a process of divine communication which began at Bethlehem!

Jan 2000   **MILLENNIUM**

The new age has dawned! We've celebrated. We've partied. We've welcomed the new millennium. But what's different?

Hopes that the 1st of January would usher in a new era of peace, justice and kindness have failed to materialise. Thankfully so also have the various doomsday scenarios sketched by secular and spiritual prophets who felt compelled to warn us that the end would be now.

Perhaps the aftermath of the celebrations, when we are waking up to the 'ordinariness' of life in the third millennium, is an appropriate time to reflect on the significance of another millennium – *the* Millennium which is highlighted in the Book of Revelation chapter 20.

No section of the Book of Revelation has been subjected to greater variety of interpretation that the paragraphs in chapter 20.1-6! So I intend to follow the safer route and focus on the symbolic, rather than any literal, meaning of the millennium.

The thousand years of Revelation 20 can be seen as 'a symbolic span of time, perfect, complete, finished, beautifully symmetrical' (Dennis Lennon). As such it represents *God's time* - which overlaps with *our time*, but is different from it. *Our time* is measured in tenses - past, present and future. Whereas

God's time transcends past, present and future: 'I am the first and the last, says the Lord God Almighty, who is and who was and who is to come' (1.8).

Jesus lived in God's time as well as in human time. His birth, life, death, resurrection and ascension were real events in our time and space. But in God's time these events are present and future as well as past! That is why we, living 2,000 years on, can speak of being crucified with Christ and of rising with Christ. That is why Christians experience *now* their acquittal (or `justification') at the future day of judgment.

As Christians we live in two time zones at once! Historical time and `millennial time'. And the challenge we face is to live our lives in historical time according to the values of millennial time! What does this mean?

Triumph of Truth

A key value of the millennial vision is public truth. We are told that during 1000 years, the Devil `could not deceive the nations any more' (20.3).

The theme of truth and falsehood is key in the Book of Revelation:

- Jesus is the faithful and true witness (3.14)

- The rider of the white horse is called `Faithful and True' (19.11)

- The martyrs were executed because they had proclaimed the truth that Jesus revealed and the word of God' (Rev. 20.4)

- John is assured that the words of the revelation he has been given are true and can be trusted (22.6)

In contrast, the dragon deceives the whole world (12.9), the second beast deceives the inhabitants of the earth (13.14), and Babylon deceives the nations with her false magic (18.23).

We today, no less than John in the late first century, are called to be faithful to the word of God and to the testimony of Jesus Christ' (1.2). To answer such a call in a world where so often `truth is on the scaffold and wrong is on the throne' can be very difficult! Even for churches and Christian agencies!

But this is where the biblical millennium encourages us to renew our commitment to communicate the Word of God as public truth. For it reminds us that Truth will ultimately triumph. Truth has power to overcome all lies, propaganda, brain washing and half truths!

Power of Prayer

Another key value of the biblical millennium is prayer. It is as priests that the martyrs rule with Christ for a thousand years (20.6). A key component of the work of a priest is praying for others, and it is probable that prayer is one of the means through which Christ and the martyrs rule the world.

Certainly in Revelation, prayer is powerful:

- Prayers of praise follow the Lamb's taking the scroll of destiny from the right hand of God seated on the throne (5.8).

- God calls for cosmic silence to listen to the prayers of his people, and when the angel-priest takes the incense, which had been mingled with the prayers, and tosses it on the earth, the impact is cataclysmic (8.3-5)!

The imagery demonstrates that `Prayer puts the believer in touch with the deepest mysteries of world processes and events' (Dennis Lennon), and suggests that John, a prisoner in the Patmos concentration camp, had access to a power greater than Caesar ruling the empire with his legions!

The biblical millennium is the doorway into the real corridors of power! It tells us that through our prayers we can share in Christ's rule and influence the headlines in tomorrow's newspapers!

Will our prayers be as central as our pentiums in planning Bible work in the 21st century?

Defeat of Death

The key event of John's millennial vision after the chaining of the Dragon, is the raising to life of the executed martyrs to rule as kings with Christ (20.4). They are no longer victims, but victors! Death has been decisively defeated (20.6)!

According to Revelation the `Man behind the Millennium' is the one who says: `I am the living one! I was dead, but now I am alive for ever and ever. I have authority over death and the world of the dead' (1.18).

So a third feature of the biblical millennium is that there is no fear of death!

This millennium is the portal of a new order where there will be no more death, no more grief or crying or pain (21.4). Just as we have recently passed through the frontier between the second and the third millennia, so the followers of Jesus will pass through death into God's nearer presence and eternal life.

During one of the most difficult times for the churches in the Soviet era, Nikita Krushchev ordered an investigation into why Christianity was not dying out in the face of the prevailing atheist philosophy. The report identified several reasons. The most telling was that Soviet Christians allowed no one to die without consolation!

In western countries today, people visit the doctor or go to hospital expecting to be healed. Few go expecting to die. Expectations of medicine are so high that death takes many people by surprise. Few are prepared to go when the last call comes. But die we all must and die we all will!

There are some signs that this western taboo against facing up to death may be weakening. One of these is the growth of the hospice movement. In all probability a new openness to death will provide us with fresh opportunities in the 21st century to communicate the Bible's message of eternal life!

So the real Millennium is much more than a date on the calendar! It's a way of life, a set of values which believes in truth, trusts in prayer and defies death!

In his novel 'The Testament', John Grisham's depiction of Rachel Lane, a young medical missionary serving a small tribe in the upper reaches of the Amazon, sets in sharp contrast the millennial values by which she lived and died with the earth-bound values of her family in the United States.

Nate O'Riley, a hard-living Washington attorney, tracks her down, but totally fails to persuade her to accept the fortune she has just inherited from her billionaire father. Some weeks later the attorney returns to try again. Only to discover that tragedy has struck. The missionary doctor has died from malaria! Grisham describes the scene as the stunned lawyer stands at her simple grave:

> Buried there was Rachel Lane, the bravest person he'd ever known because she had absolutely no fear of death. She welcomed it. She was at peace, her soul finally with the Lord, her body forever lying among the people she loved.

Rachel Lane had entered *the* Millennium!

YEAR THREE

Feb 2000   # FESTIVAL

In the Bible, the festivals and assemblies which brought God's people together play a key role in the life of the community of faith. We learn this especially in Old Testament and in the Gospels where we read of pilgrims 'going up' to Jerusalem to celebrate the great Jewish festivals.

This year is a 'festival year' for the UBS, for it is World Assembly year. From 10-14 October, Midrand, South Africa, will become the UBS 'Jerusalem' as all the Bible Societies gather there. World Assemblies are important because they set the strategic directions of the movement for its next phase. World Assembly 2000 will be doubly important because it will also determine what the UBS will do, and how it will do it, for well into the new century.

So it's vital that at Midrand we get it right! That's why the World Assembly Task Force and the Structure Review Group are actively seeking to get Bible Societies involved beforehand in *making* the decisions which together they will be *taking* at the Assembly. A pre-Assembly consultation with Bible Societies through telephone and postal surveys has already taken place. Now, in the first three months of this year representatives of Bible Societies are meeting in regional gatherings to prepare further for Midrand. These gatherings will provide forums of consultation on tentative proposals relating to our UBS identity and ethos and UBS governance which have come out of the surveys already referred to. The hope is that through this process we will find the common ground which will enable the Assembly to become a genuine manifestation of unity.

Harmony and unity

I have been reflecting on Psalm 133. It is one of the 'Songs of Ascent' (Psalms 120-134) which were probably sung by pilgrims 'going up' to Jerusalem to celebrate one or other of the great Old Testament festivals. Psalm 133 delights in harmony among faith brothers and sisters. I have been so impressed how relevant it is as we prepare for Midrand! This poetic and liturgical celebration of unity in diversity provides us with powerful biblical inspiration as we work our way towards genuine, broad consensus on matters which could so easily divide rather than unite us.

Psalm 133 tells us that unity is a blessing which is beautiful, bountiful and fruitful.

This ought to stop us in our tracks! For Christians do not have the best reputation when it comes to unity! Mark Twain, the American novelist, used to say he put a dog and a cat in a cage together to see if they could get along. They did. So next he put in a bird, a pig and a goat. They also got along. Then he put in the cage a Baptist, a Presbyterian and a Catholic, and soon there was not a living thing left!

'Living together in a way that evokes the glad song of Psalm 133 is one of the great and arduous tasks before Christ's people,' writes Eugene Peterson in *A Long Obedience in the Same Direction*. 'Nothing requires more attention and energy. It is easier to do almost anything else. It is far easier to deal with people as problems to be solved than to have anything to do with them in community.'

So don't let us be under any illusion about the challenge which faces us! But we can take encouragement from the fact that the motif in the background of Psalm 133 is the family. For, if families sometimes fight, they are always at their best when they stay together and become centres of love and joy.!

Oil and dew

Alongside the family motif, the psalm employs two striking images. The first is anointing oil (v.2). The second heavy dew (v.3). Taken together, they signify that unity is a gift from God. The anointing oil ran *down* Aaron's head and beard, and the dew comes *down* from heaven. The fact that our unity comes from above makes prayer a vital part of our World Assembly preparation.

Taken separately these images illustrate that Christian unity is not an end in itself. It is much more than cosy feelings of togetherness.

· Oil suggests that unity is seen in our serving others. When Aaron was anointed high priest he was consecrated to serve his fellows. The aim to achieve unity at the World Assembly sees unity not as a terminus, but as a hub from which we will serve one another, the world and, above all, God.

· Dew hints that unity is expressed in empowering others. In the Bible lands heavy dews (those of Mount Hermon are particularly copious) provide moisture which can make the desert bloom. World Assembly 2000 will be a 'working assembly'; it's aim will be not only to inspire participants, but also to invest in them so that they will return to their Bible Societies enabled to meet challenges they had previously turned away from.

Both word pictures underline that unity is possible only if first there is community – 'a place where each person is taken seriously, learns to trust others, depend on others, be compassionate with others, rejoice with others' (Eugene Peterson). Let us all pray that the Midrand Assembly may be a great experience of Christian community at its best!

Finally, I want to stress that the World Assembly will be for those who are not there as well as for those who will! Unfortunately there can be only a maximum of two representatives from each Bible Society physically present in Midrand. Direct participation will be open only to a small minority of the thousands of members of our global family composed of board members, staff members, prayer partners, supporters, volunteers and many more. But I do hope that the majority who cannot be present at Midrand may discover a sense of participation by actively helping with the preparations and, later, with the follow-up. There is no doubt that the Assembly will affect us all. So let all of us do what we can to influence it and implement it!

In conclusion, I would like to return to the regional gatherings. May they be occasions when together we will re-consecrate ourselves to one another and to the Bible cause! May we go back to our Bible Societies more committed than ever before to enable the Word of God to run along the streets and alleys, the country roads and paths of our national territories! And may the good seed of the Scriptures which hopefully will reach more people as a result of our meetings, be enabled to germinate quickly because the soil into which it falls will have been watered by the dew of heaven!

March 2000   **GRIEF**

This letter is being written in the departure lounge of Abuja airport, Nigeria. I am on my way back to the World Service Center after attending the funeral services of Revd Gaius Musa and Revd Dr Stephen Niyang, who as all of you will now know, were tragically killed in the Kenya Airways Airbus accident at Abidjan on 30 January.

As I look back over the events of the last two days, and, indeed, over the entire period since tragedy struck our two brothers and 167 others on Flight 431, I find myself bombarded by a collage of memories and impressions.

`In days filled with trouble I search for you'
I am still reacting with shock and grief at losing in such tragic circumstances two of our key Bible Society workers in Africa, both of whom, I believe, were

poised to achieve even greater things for the Bible cause had they lived. This sense of frustration is compounded by the loss in the same accident of two of SIL-Wycliffe leaders in Africa, Robert and Ruth Chapman, whose family have close links with the Canadian Bible Society. All four perished while actively serving the Bible cause in Africa and at the height of their powers. It's extremely difficult to understand why God allowed four of the best Bible workers in Africa to be removed from ministries which are so vital for the coming of God's Kingdom in Africa.

However, this spirit of frustration and questioning has been to a large extent mitigated by the strong faith of our African friends which found expression in the funeral services. I am coming away from these services deeply impressed by the faith of Sarah Musa and Ruth Niyang, their immediate and extended families and the many hundreds of their friends who attended the funerals. This faith in a loving God who is able to overrule disasters is enabling them to absorb with amazing resilience the tragedy which has engulfed them and to find great comfort and an extraordinary sense of divine purpose in what has happened.

`Away from the body and at home with the Lord'

Both services took place in central Nigeria. Gaius' funeral was held on Friday 11 February in his home village of Angwal, in Kaduna State, about two and a half hours' drive north-east from Abuja, the new federal capital city of Nigeria. The service was held in the local sanctuary of the Evangelical Church of West Africa (ELWA), a denomination founded by what was the Sudan Interior Mission which Gaius had served as Director of Personnel and Administration until his appointment as General Secretary of the Bible Society of Nigeria in 1996. The well sized building was packed beyond capacity with large crowds gathered outside. Although it was clearly a funeral service, there was no gloom. A note of triumph pervaded the atmosphere, tellingly capturing the early Christians' sense of victory in the face of death. It was a great privilege for me to express the sympathy of our global UBS family and to assure the family and the congregation of our prayers. David Bolade, National President of the Bible Society of Nigeria, and Daniel Bitrus, Anglophone African Regional Secretary, who had coordinated the identification of the bodies in Abidjan and their return to Nigeria, also brought messages of condolence and comfort. At the close of the service, the congregation, led by a Boys' Brigade band, walked with the casket the few hundred yards to Gaius' family home - where his aged father still lives - for interment in the family land.

`Living is Christ and dying is gain'

Stephen's service took place the following day. The day began at 8.00 a.m. as a crowd of many hundreds gathered in the cool morning air outside the mortuary of Jos University Teaching Hospital, while the women sang spontaneously and beautifully Hausa Christian songs of hope and comfort. About 9.30 a.m. the cortege led by a police escort and followed by long procession of cars and minibuses set out for the hour's drive through the open savannah countryside of Plateau State to the village of Pushit. The local church of the Church of Christ in Nigeria (COCIN) – which was originally the fruit of the Sudan United Mission - serves a group of villages, including Stephen's home community of Vodni, where he would later be interred. The COCIN church has a large sanctuary in Pushit, and it was filled to overflowing. During the service Ruth, Stephen's widow, gave a remarkably composed testimony to the vital witness of Stephen as a husband and a father. Again, David, Daniel and I brought messages from the Bible Society family.

`He taught me a new song'

A feature of both services was the prominence of hymn singing. No one can fail to visit any African church service and fail to be moved by the beautiful harmonious singing. But singing seems to be especially significant at African funerals. In addition to congregational singing, a variety of choirs sang pieces expressing the solidarity of God's people at a time of bereavement and communicating the comfort of God's love. Africans are born singers. They really enjoy singing and know how to make their music serve the Kingdom of God. It was wonderful to witness them do so on this occasion!

`God is our shelter and strength…. So we will not be afraid!'

I've already referred to the great faith of our African brothers and sisters in the face of death. But I feel that this was so prominent that I should say a little more about it. African faith may be simple, but it is strong as a rock, and enables believers to meet tragedies of life head-on. I did not hear one whisper over the past two days questioning God's love or God's wisdom. Although obviously there was deep grief, the doubts which so often surface among Western Christians when they have to face similar disasters, were apparently totally absent. `God does not make mistakes' was reiterated several times. Again and again, the vast congregations celebrated the fact that Gaius and Stephen had `gone to glory' and were now perfectly fulfilled in higher service.

`Rulers…. are God's servants'

Another impressive factor was the presence and participation of civil, legal and political leaders, including Jerry Gana, a cabinet minister in the federal government, who spoke with great conviction of the Christian hope of eternal life. The voluntary presence of such dignitaries reflects both the prominence of Christians in Nigeria's return to democracy and also the high esteem in which the Bible Society of Nigeria is held throughout the country.

`Jesus wept'

The Africans' ability to stand in awe of death and their ready consciousness of eternity as well as time, were also prominent in the proceedings. Time was not a constraint! The `waking services' held the day before the funeral lasted up to three hours. The funeral services were somewhat shorter, but only because the church leaders had agreed they should end by mid afternoon so as to allow mourners who had come a long way to travel home during day light. Many hundreds of people had taken, or were given, long hours off their work to honour the dead and comfort the living. Personally I found this a healthy counter-balance to many western funerals which are carried out with almost clinical precision in minimal time and with maximum efficiency.

My final reflection is the fact that Gaius and Stephen's deaths are the first air travel fatalities suffered by Bible Society or UBS personnel in over 50 years of flying and a vast number of air journeys. Although this is little comfort to the Musa and Niyang families in their grievous loss, it is, I believe something for which we should be truly thankful. So as we grieve for our two Nigerian brothers, let us also thank the Lord for the quite extraordinary travelling mercies he has granted us over the years, and let us continue to acknowledge our dependence on his goodness and love as travel by varying forms of transport is constantly undertaken. Cicero the Roman poet said: `Great things the gods take care of, small things they neglect'. Let us thank God that the testimony of the Word of God is so different!

> - *We know that in all things God works for good with those who love him, those whom he has called according to his purpose.* (Romans 8.28)

> - *Who, then, can separate us from the love of Christ? Can trouble do it, or hardship or persecution or hunger or poverty or danger or death? …. No, in all these things we have complete victory through him who loved us.* (Romans 8.35,37)

Aromatherapy is a practice which comes from ancient Egypt, of using essential oils extracted from flowers and plants to heal, soothe and refresh the human body, mind and spirit. We are told that smell is the sense most intimately connected to our emotions, affecting that part of the brain which controls our feelings.

Aromatherapy has been revived in recent years. Slogans like `making sense of scents' and `get well with smell' are common in the growing range of literature devoted to it. Sometimes it appears in a New Age dress which links the essential oils yielding the scents with the `life force' of the plants from which the oils are extracted.

But the New Age connections don't make the use of perfumes wrong! Most of us find the use of perfume in every day life pleasant and attractive. And we are aware that incense is used in many Christian worship traditions – a practice going back to the Tabernacle and Temple of the Old Testament.

In addition, we find that the New Testament uses the metaphor of scent in ways which even permit us to speak of *aromatheology*! This month I'd like to suggest that a little aromatheology may be good for us!

Let's look at three key New Testament texts which relate to aromatheology:

-   Eph 5.2: *Live in love as Christ loved us and gave himself up for us, a fragrant offering and sacrifice to God.* (NRSV)

-   2 Cor 2.14-16: *I am grateful that God always makes it possible for Christ to lead us to victory. God also helps us spread the knowledge about Christ everywhere, and this knowledge is like the smell of perfume. In fact God thinks of us as a perfume that brings Christ to everyone.* (CEV)

-   Phil 4.18: *They [i.e. your gifts] are like a sweet-smelling offering to God, a sacrifice that is acceptable and pleasing to him.* (GNB)

These biblical passages use perfume as a metaphor to describe activities which are pleasing to God. And all of them occur in contexts which are not dissimilar to the situations we often face in Bible work. This is why a closer look at each might encourage us.

Consecration

The immediate context of the Ephesian passage is an apostolic command to practise love in the Christian community. The wider context is the challenge to demonstrate in practice the essential unity of Jewish and Gentile believers. In either case, the model presented is the example of the sheer love of Christ in offering his life for us on the cross. The perfume here I love – *agape* love, love for the undeserving, love which doesn't count the cost, love which overcomes cultural differences and bridges confessional divisions.

The UBS is a bit like the churches to which this letter was originally written. We, like they, are grappling with how to express our fundamental unity in Christ and in the service of his Word, in a context of many cultures and different confessions. It is not an easy task! Ethnic prejudices are strong, misunderstanding of other confessions can be deep-seated. But agape love prevents such tensions festering! It is as we, coming from our different cultures and churches, accept and love one another simply because Christ has loved and accepted us all, that we can work together in harmony. It is as we consecrate ourselves to one another that we consecrate ourselves to God. By transcending cultural, racial, social and confessional differences in the service of Christ, the UBS is doing a beautiful work for God!

Concentration

The context of the Corinthian text is strained relationships, the trauma of recent physical dangers and deep anxiety about the safety of a colleague. In the previous chapter Paul alludes to his perilous experiences in Asia Minor (1.8-11), and immediately preceding the aroma passage he shares with his readers the acute distress he felt when he did not find Titus in Troas (2.12-13). The 'but' with which 2.14 begins in formal equivalent translations suggests Paul is pausing to regain his perspective as a Christian missionary. He encourages himself – and us – by the reminder that whenever we are active in the service of the Good News, 'God thinks of us as a perfume that brings Christ to everyone' (v.16, CEV).

Like Paul, we in Bible Society service sometimes find ourselves beset by difficulties. These difficulties can arise from a range of situations.

- The frustration of trying to meet enormous Scripture needs with meagre resources.
- The exhaustion that can come from having to deal with obstinate government officials.
- The tensions that arise from misunderstandings with the churches.

And there are many more, all of which in the 'heat of the day' can magnify themselves in our perception to grotesque proportions. It is in moments like these that Paul's example becomes so helpful. By concentrating on the beauty of the essence of what we do – for Bible Societies no less than the apostle are spreading the knowledge about Christ everywhere – we regain perspective and recover our poise.

Co-operation

The context in Philippians 4 is Paul's closing greetings to a community of believers he felt very close to. He had given them much; he had brought them the gospel and had helped them grow in their newly found faith. As a result they were deeply grateful to him, and expressed their gratitude by sending monetary gifts to support his apostolic work. In the verse in view he thanks the Philippians and tells them that he regards their gifts as a fragrant offering to God.

The giving and receiving between Paul and the Philippians finds an echo in the mutual support which is a key feature of life in our UBS fellowship. Like Paul's partnership, ours also involves the exchange of money and more than money. Some Bible Societies contribute money which others in our fellowship receive. But much more than finance is shared. So also are goods and services, prayer, encouragement, advice etc. The UBS is essentially a co-operative venture made possible by the sacrificial sharing of a wide range of resources. Let us not forget that these gifts which we share with one another, like the Philippians' gifts to Paul, become something God finds beautiful and attractive.

So we practise aromatheology in the UBS as we:
- Consecrate ourselves to one another, laying aside all selfish agendas
- Concentrate on the essence of our mission, refusing to be distracted
- Co-operate together, rejecting all thoughts that to receive is inferior

As we practice aromatheology, we become the most beautiful perfume the world has ever known!

It is commonly acknowledged that our natural body scents are caused by what we eat. With that fact in mind, another biblical allusion to the metaphor of scent takes on a new significance. This reference is found in the first part of the prophetic portrait of the Messiah in Isaiah 11: `His greatest joy will be to obey the Lord' (v.11, CEV). The literal rendering of the Hebrew is: `His smell is the fear of the Lord'. Jesus said that his food was to do the will of him who sent him (John 4.34). And for us it is no different. It is as we make doing the will of God our meat and drink that our lives will be permeated with the scent of Jesus!

An old adage tells us that `actions speak louder than words'. It is used most frequently when our intentions are not matched by our deeds. Perhaps this maxim is most often applied in the UBS today to the participation of women – in national Bible Society Boards and UBS Committees, on one hand, and in the senior staff of both Bible Societies and UBS Service Centers on the other.

There have been some fine words on this issue. Listen for a moment to the lofty rhetoric of the Mississauga World Assembly in 1996! There as a Fellowship we committed ourselves *'to ensure the full and equal participation of women in Bible Society work and their appointment to boards, committees and staff leadership positions'*.

But actions have not followed! In September 1999, UBSEC received a report indicating that only 16% of UBS senior staff positions were filled by women, and that on national Bible Society Boards men outnumbered women by 5 to 1 .

Why is our Fellowship reluctant to move decisively on this issue?

I believe the root of the problem lies with us men! At the moment men form a majority in most Bible Society and UBS decision-taking bodies, so they hold the key to the speedy implementation of the Mississauga challenge. Am I right in sensing a certain lack of conviction among men on this issue? It's not that UBS men are against greater participation of women. But many of us tend to wait for it to evolve naturally, rather than taking positive steps to encourage it to happen in our life time.

I am convinced that this laissez-faire response to Mississauga will not change until we gain a new biblical and theological insight into the importance of women in the Kingdom of God. So this month I wish to invite all of us – men and women – to reconsider the Bible's message about the relation of women and men.

Equality

In the Book of Genesis there are two accounts of creation, one in 1.1-2.4a and another in 2.4b-3.24. The first stresses that humankind was created `male and female', and is totally devoid of any suggestion that one gender is more dignified than the other, for both were created `in the image of God'. The second account in 2.18-25 provides `the only full account of the creation of women in ancient near eastern literature' (NIV Study Bible). God created men and women for partnership.

Sadly this vision of pristine equality became sullied by what theologians call the Fall. One of the direct results was patriarchy (Genesis 3.16); another was polygamy (Genesis 4.19). In both instances women became the losers. And the following pages of the Old Testament reflect a patriarchal social structure where only the man had legal status with corresponding rights and duties. Nevertheless, even in the Old Testament there are outstanding exceptions in which women such as Ruth, Deborah, Rahab, Hannah, Huldah and Esther provide outstanding leadership.

The New Testament introduces a paradigm shift, reflecting Jesus' revolutionary attitude to women, summed up by St Paul: `Faith in Christ Jesus is what makes each of you equal with each other, whether you are a Jew or a Greek, a slave or a free person, a man or a woman.' (Galatians 3.28, CEV). Here is some concrete evidence of this paradigm shift. There were...

- Women among the disciples of Jesus (Luke 8.1-3)
- Women prophets in the early church (Acts 21.9)
- Female preachers of the Word (Acts 18.1-4, 24-28; Philippians 4.1-3)
- Lady leaders of local churches (Acts 12.12; 16.11-15,40; Romans 16.3-5)
- Women church workers (Romans 16.1-16)

However, there is unmistakable evidence that the church also reflected the prevailing patriarchy of 1st century society (1 Corinthians 11.3-10; 14.33b-36; 1 Timothy 2.8-15; Ephesians 5.22-24; 1 Peter 3.1-6). But there is little doubt that women on becoming Christians began to experience a degree of liberation unknown to them hitherto.

Complementarity

The second feature of the Bible's view on women and men is that they have complementary roles as well as identical roles. In other words, their equality is not to be totally equated with similarity. If we think of male and female roles as constituting a spectrum, we would discover a large degree of overlap (i.e. identical roles) in the centre of the spectrum. But as you move out from the centre you would encounter mainly female roles towards one end and mainly male roles towards the other, while at the extremities the roles are exclusively female or male.

In 1 Corinthians 11.1-16, St Paul articulates both the complementary roles of men and women and their mutual inter-dependence. In verse 3 he stresses complementarity: `Now I want you to know that Christ is the head over all men, and a man is the head over a woman. But God is the head over Christ' (CEV). The comparison of the man-woman association with the God-Christ relationship suggests that `headship' here symbolises mutual service, not inequality.

In verse 11 St Paul adds the thought of mutual inter-dependence: `In our life in the Lord, however, woman is not independent of man, nor is man independent of woman' (GNB). (However, in addition to stating this principle, he cautions women against flouting convention by praying in public without a head covering.)

There is a striking instance of complementarity in the gospels where Martha's confession of Jesus as the Christ in John 11.27 parallels Peter's confession in Matthew 16.17.

It is not too dogmatic to say that the complementary roles of men and women provide the essential chemistry of true community in both the church and society.

Is not the challenge we face in our Bible Societies and the UBS, to exhibit this biblical complementarity of men and women in our governance and service structures.. Without a deep conviction that such complementarity is God's will, we will never be able to reduce the perceived threat that women in leadership tend to present to male-oriented traditions. Nor will we be able to broaden, deepen and enrich the prevailing male understanding of Christian community and fellowship.

Creativity

Because the Bible is the story of God's dealing with real people in live communities it is, of necessity, historically and culturally conditioned. Because God speaks in order that people might understand, he contextualises his message in the culture of the people to whom it was originally sent. At the same time, God's message challenged its first hearers to redeem and sanctify their culture by living in that culture a life of faith and obedience. So we can say the Bible is both pro-culture and counter-culture.

As we today read and experience the Bible we also find ourselves being challenged. First of all, we are called on to distinguish between the message and its cultural wrapping. And then we are invited to express the message in terms which our 21st century culture will be able to understand. We need to remind ourselves constantly that God has not given us the Bible as a self-contained book of theoretical ideas, but as a covenant text which calls for our creative response.

Our responsibility is to engage creatively with this text, wrestling with its inner tensions between message and context, to discover where it is leading us today. Nowhere is this task more demanding than in relation to the participation of women! We have already seen the challenge the passage on head coverings (1 Corinthians 11) presents.

There are many more such tensions built into Scripture, for God wants us to engage with his Word, personally and communally. Here are another two examples:

- Yahweh was known as `the God of Abraham, Isaac and Jacob', yet it was their wives that he took into his confidence when revealing the future of their children, e.g. Sarah (Genesis 21.1-10) and Rebekah (Genesis 25.19-26).

- Despite the testimony of women having no legal standing (they were treated like minors), Jesus chose women to be the first witnesses of his resurrection (Matthew 28.9-10; Luke 24.1-10). Yet when the early church came to replace Judas, only men were proposed (Acts 1.23) despite one of the essential qualifications for the vacancy being a witness to Jesus' resurrection (Acts 1.22)!

The key to engaging with Scripture is:

- First, to recognise that it comes to us in narrative form – it is God's master-story.

- Second, to learn to indwell this story in our imagination and come to experience the story as speaking to us.

- Third, to submit our situation, with all its problems and opportunities, to the text of Scripture, praying for fresh insight into its practical relevance for us and for a renewed faith to follow in the direction it points.

This will undoubtedly involve creativity and innovation on our part, for God's Word, when it is heard, is always active and radical. However, fortunately God does not leave us to ourselves in this. He has given us the Holy Spirit to lead us into truth. So we *can* expect the meaning and relevance of the Scriptures to become increasingly clear to us.

The development of a Christian conscience on slavery after 18 centuries of Christian history demonstrates this fact. The challenge we face today regarding the status and role of women is surely to ask God to help us to make explicit in our culture today the appropriate biblical principles which are implicit, but not necessarily explicit, in the Biblical narrative.

Let us all seek to do this, praying for the guidance of the Holy Spirit and for the resultant enrichment of our UBS fellowship!

June 2000   **GRACE**

One of the most compelling books I have read recently is Philip Yancy's *What's so Amazing about Grace?* With great poignancy Yancy presents repeated and compelling examples of the loss of grace as the great motivator among today's Christians. Although he writes against a North American background, the evidence he cites can be replicated in many other parts of the world.

Why is it that harsh legalism and cold formalism are hardening the spiritual arteries of the Body of Christ? Why are many churches in danger of becoming reformatories of law rather than renewal centres of grace?

The answer must be: Because they've lost a sense of the wonder of God's mercy!

This can happen all too easily. How effortlessly we slip out of the disposition of the tax collector into the role of the Pharisee! (Luke 18.9-14) Too easily we find ourselves thinking we are better than others and able to look down on everyone else!

If this is our attitude, St Paul's straight talking to the Church in Rome is a message for us. In that church there was internal strife between the `strong' and the `weak' over matters of diet and calendar. (Romans 14-15) The weak censured the strong and the strong despised the weak. The apostle urges them to accept one another for the simple reason that God accepts them both! (Romans 14.3)

Triangular grace

Triangular grace (from God to us all, from us to others and others to us) is a prerequisite of Christian harmony and cooperation, and something we should covet and pray for as we approach the World Assembly in October. In the nature of the event there will be differences of opinion among us during the Assembly. But if we are determined to welcome all whom God has accepted, then those of us who go to Midrand will be able to cherish one another and overcome partisan attitudes to achieve consensus.

Have you noticed that in the gospels there is an almost complete absence of the word *holiness*? This seems very strange in light of the commandment `Be holy because I, the LORD your God, am holy' which was given in the Old Testament (Leviticus 19.2 and 11.4) and validated in the New Testament epistles (1 Peter 1.15,16). But on further reflection it seems clear that Jesus deliberately avoided this term – which was central to the worldview of the Pharisees and Scribes - because it had come to mean self-righteous exclusion of others (including the poor and the sick) on the basis of a complicated ritual system of `clean' (the same as us) and `unclean' (different from us).

Perhaps this is why Jesus replaced the commandment `Be holy...' with `Be merciful, just as your Father is merciful'. (Luke 6.36). For Jesus, rejection, exclusion and disdain are non-starters in lives motivated and captivated by grace!

Finally, a couple of questions about the World Assembly: First question - will the hymn `Amazing grace' be sung at the World Assembly? Answer - I don't know, for the musical program is still in preparation. An assembly without the song could still be a great success. But an assembly without grace can only fail! So the second and more important question is – will amazing grace be the dynamic of our fellowship at the Assembly? Let us all pray that it will!

July 2000   BIBLE TRANSLATION

Bible translation is a specialist activity, it can sometimes be overshadowed by other Bible Society activities which are more visible, like distribution, Scripture engagement, and fundraising. But the Mississauga document reminds us that `Translation has been the backbone of Bible Society ministries, and it is still a key element in our mission.'

This is at the forefront of my mind at the moment because I am writing this month's letter from the UBS Translators' Triennial Workshop in Torremolinos, Spain. The workshop has such a fascinating program allowing participants to review and reflect on some of the latest insights in linguistic and biblical studies, that I am truly sorry to be here only for two days!

We learn about the earliest example of Scripture translation in Nehemiah 8.8. There we are told that certain Levites `gave an oral translation of God's Law and explained it so that the people could understand it.' (GNB). The `people' were returned Jewish exiles. They had gathered in a square near Jerusalem's Water Gate to celebrate the Law, or *Torah*.

The wall of Jerusalem had been rebuilt and the city gates put in place (6.15; 7.1). The time had come for a popular reading of the Torah. But many of the returned exiles had lost their Hebrew in Babylonia where they adopted the Aramaic of their conquerors. So the Levites translated the Hebrew Scriptures as they read.

Careful study of this fascinating incident reveals that Nehemiah 8 is not only a report, but also a reflection on the significance of Scripture translation. It presents three simple, yet basic, presuppositions of such translation. The first is that:

God speaks

'They asked Ezra, the priest and prophet of the Law which the Lord had given Israel through Moses, to get the book of the Law' (8.1).

The people see the Law as a message which in a unique sense comes from the Lord. They believed that God communicates through language.

This idea is captured today in the marketing title of the Spanish Popular Version – *Dios habla hoy* – 'God speaks today'. Fundamental to the task of Bible translation is the fact that God speaks to us through the Scriptures.

God spoke to the people before the Water Gate. He did this because the Levites were able to translate the language of the Scriptures into a language which the people spoke and understood.

These returned exiles were to be the first of many who would receive God's Word in their own language. Over a century later the entire Hebrew canon was translated into Greek so that the growing number of Hellenistic Jews of the *diaspora* could hear God speak to them. A few more centuries and we find the New Testament Scriptures being written, not in the classical Greek of academics, but in the *koine* Greek of the market place, the popular language of the eastern Roman Empire. These New Testament Scriptures tell us that Jesus Christ commissioned his followers to make disciples of all ethno-linguistic groups (Matthew 28.19: 'peoples' [GNB]; 'nations' [NRSV]) and envisions a future world order where God will be praised in every language (Revelation 7.9; cf 5.9 and 14.6).

One of the factors which distinguishes Christianity from other world faiths is its commitment to translation. We have no holy language! Others do. If you wish to become deeply initiated into other faiths, you have to learn the language of their Scriptures. But to hear God speak, Christians believe it is not necessary to learn God's language simply because he already speaks ours! The great task of Bible translators is to help God to speak more languages and so enable many more people to hear his voice! This brings us to the second presupposition, which is that:

Believers hear

'There in the square by the Water Gate he [Ezra] read the Law to them from dawn until noon, and they all listened attentively.' (Nehemiah 8.3)

In the Bible hearing is believing.

The *Shema* (Hebrew for `hear'), taken from Deuteronomy 6.4-9 (`Hear, O Israel: the Lord our God, the Lord is one. Love the Lord your God with all your heart and with all your soul and with all your strength....' NIV) has become the Jewish confession of faith (cf. Matthew 22.37-38; Mark 12.29-30; Luke 10.27).

St Paul's key question to the Galatian defectors was: `Tell me this one thing, did you receive God's Spirit by doing what the Law requires or by hearing the gospel and believing it?' (Galatians 3.2 GNB) Tom Torrance, who taught Christian dogmatics at Edinburgh University for many years - and whose father was an early American Bible Society worker in China - says that both Israel and the Church are called to be acoustic communities, communities which exist as they hear and respond to the Word of God.

In fact, more people in Bible times heard than read the Scriptures! Notice *how* the people gathered before the Water Gate heard.

First, they heard in *adoration*. `As soon as he opened the book, they all stood up. Ezra said, "Praise the Lord, the great God!" All the people raised their arms in the air and answered, "Amen. Amen." They knelt in worship with their faces to the ground. Then they arose and stood in their places, and the following Levites explained the Law to them.' For them, to hear the Law was to be granted an encounter with God!

Have we today lost this sense of expectancy?

Do we expect to meet the transcendent God when we hear his Word?

Second, they heard with *celebration*. At first, they wept (Nehemiah 8.9), probably from a mixture of mass emotion and a sense of personal guilt. But Nehemiah, Ezra and the Levites told the crowd: `This day is holy to the Lord your God, so you are not to mourn and cry. Now go home and have a feast!' (vv.9,10).

So often today, the first time publication in a language of a New Testament or a Bible is an occasion for great joy and celebration among the speakers of the language concerned. And rightly so!

Bible Society ministry is joyful! The gospel means `good news'! To hear God speak is like participating in a feast, not a funeral! This is why Bible Society people should be encouragers of the people of God.

Third, they heard with *compassion*. Their celebration of the Word was humanitarian, not hedonistic. `Have a feast!' said Ezra. But he went on to say: `Share your food and wine with those who haven't enough' (v.10). And the writer observes: `So all the people went home and ate and drank joyfully and shared what they had with others, because they understood what had been read to them' (v.12).

True hearing of God's Word results in caring for the less fortunate. One of the reasons why many Bible Societies are producing Scriptures for use in holistic programs of the churches and mission agencies is to enable those who benefit from such programs to discover the motivation of those who help them.

Fourth, they heard in *community*. It is interesting that in a culture where worship was regarded as being largely an adult male preserve, women and children were full participants (v.2). Both women and children constitute strategic audiences today.

- Literacy among women is one of the recognised indicators of social and political improvement.
- Children under 18 compose between 30 and 50% of our total audience in many countries.

All of this serves to remind us that there is a great need to produce Scriptures for men and women, for adults and for children. Our challenge is not only to translate the Word of God into all languages, but also to ensure that the translated Word engages every section of the social stratum of the cultures into whose languages the Word enters via translation.

The final presupposition of Scripture translation is that:

People ask

It's important to note that the large gathering of people in Jerusalem took place at the people's request: 'They asked Ezra... to get the book of the Law' (v.1). Further, the meeting took place in a public square, not in the temple. The temple had a special place in God's purposes and was of great importance to the community, yet this key event in the nation's rebirth took place outside its walls. 'The temple with its ritual was made for the sake of the Torah, not Torah for the sake of the temple' (Frederick Carlson Holmgren).

If we adapt this quotation about the temple to the church, we can discern the rationale of the Bible Societies' view of their role in relation to the churches. We serve all churches, but are owned by none. Why? Because the Bible does not belong to any single confession or denomination. It belongs to all.

Indeed, there's a sense in which it belongs also to people outside the churches. Such people on occasion do ask for Scriptures. And the Bible Societies have a duty to respond positively where requests come from people who - like many in our postmodern world - are disillusioned with the church, and who the churches are unable (and sometimes, alas!, unwilling) to reach. Bible Societies may be uniquely positioned to communicate the Scriptures to them!

In my letter of last May I emphasised that we need more women involved in Bible Society work at all levels. This is particularly true in translation work where men seem to be unusually dominant. I hope that this month's meditation on Nehemiah 8 may encourage some of the ladies within our global Bible Society family to consider Scripture translation as a calling.

August 2000   WILD GEESE

While visiting Vancouver, Canada, last month, I was taken by some friends to the George Reifel Waterfowl Refuge on Westham Island which lies in the estuary of the Fraser River. The refuge is a `wetland' location where the dykes are wooded, providing an environment of marsh and trees which attracts many water birds.

Among the many birds I saw that Sunday afternoon were Canadian geese. The sight of these beautiful wild birds reminded me that geese provided the ancient Celtic Christians with a striking image of the Church. The Celts were very conscious that the Church is a community rather than a series of individuals, and they saw a parable in the flock behaviour of geese.

Visitors to the tiny island of Iona in the Hebrides - the cradle of early Scottish Christianity - can obtain in the Abbey bookshop a small poster containing five `Lessons from Geese'. These lessons are relevant, not only to the Church, but to any Christian community, like the Bible Societies, which works within and alongside the Church. This month I wish to share with you these lessons - lightly contextualised in our UBS reality - because I believe they have much to say to us as we prepare for the World Assembly, which is, arguably, the most tangible expression there is of the UBS in community.

1 It's easier together

As each bird flaps its wings, it creates an uplift for others behind it. In fact, geese in V-formation have over 70% greater flying range than when flying alone.

Lesson: Bible Societies which share a common direction and sense of common purpose can get more quickly to where they want to go.

2 It's harder alone

Whenever a goose flies out of formation, it quickly feels drag and tries to get back into position. Geese in formation fly 75% faster than a single goose.

Lesson: It's harder for Bible Societies to do something alone than to do it together.

3 It's important to share

When the lead goose gets tired, it rotates back into formation and another goose flies at the head of the V.

Lesson: Shared leadership and interdependence gives us each a chance to lead as well as opportunities to rest. As a flat, networked organisation, with many joint endeavours, the UBS offers most Bible Societies an opportunity to provide a measure of leadership to the wider fellowship.

4 It's powerful to encourage

The geese flying in formation honk from behind to encourage those up front to keep up their speed.

Lesson: At the World Assembly let us make sure our honking is encouraging and not discouraging!

5 It's great to care

When a goose gets sick or wounded and falls, two geese leave the formation and stay with it until it revives or dies. Then they catch up with the flock.

Lesson: In our UBS fellowship we commit ourselves to stand by one another in difficult times as well as in good.

The wild goose is a Celtic symbol of the Holy Spirit. As we prepare for the World Assembly, let us pray that that event may be an experience of the Holy Spirit in community, creating new ideas, leading us into the unknown future and granting us the power to do the will of God.

PS Before and after my visit to the Westham Island waterfowl refuge, I attended nearby South Delta Baptist Church. A memorable phrase of the preacher has stayed with me, perhaps because it reinforced one of the lessons of the parable of the wild geese. The phrase was this:

`Looking for what's wrong, prevents us from seeing what's right'.

September 2000 WATER OF LIFE

Water is assuredly one of the most graphic images in human literature. This is not surprising since water fulfills essential roles in fostering and maintaining life. Water germinates seeds, irrigates crops, satisfies thirst and generates power.

One of the most colourful metaphors of water in the Bible is found in Ezekiel 47. There the prophetic vision pictures a small stream bursting forth from the Jerusalem temple court in ever widening and deepening volume until it becomes a mighty river, cascading down the wadis of the Judean hill country until it reaches the Dead Sea in the Jordan valley, over 3,500 feet (1,000 metres) below.

This prophetic picture anticipates John's vision in chapter 22 of the Book of Revelation of the river of life, as well as resonating with many other New Testament allusions to water.

There are two specific allusions which I find particularly helpful in interpreting Ezekiel's vision. These are:

- `Christ loved the Church and gave himself up for her in order to make her holy by cleansing her with the washing of water by the word'* (Ephesians 5.26, NRSV).

- `He saved us, not because of any works of righteousness which we had done, but according to his mercy, by the water of rebirth and renewal of the Holy Spirit'* (Titus 3.5).

The first of these references uses water as a symbol of the Word of God; the second, of Baptism and the Holy Spirit.

I believe that Ezekiel's dynamic vision of the flowing river is helpfully understood if we see it as portraying the powerful impact made on human lives when the Word of God is empowered by the Spirit of God.

Reports of Bible work today, as well as in the past, yield countless examples of the powerful influence of the Word of God on human life and culture. But this month, it might be helpful to seek evidence of this among ourselves, by examining the extent to which that same Word is impacting our individual lives and the corporate life of our Bible Societies and of the UBS. Such self-examination is appropriate at all times, but surely it is especially so immediately prior to a World Assembly. The Midrand Assembly will be asked to produce a strategic direction to guide our Fellowship for the next four years as we all seek to increase the number of people worldwide who own, use and value the Bible.

Surely it will be difficult, indeed, impossible, for us to achieve this aim unless all members of our Bible Society family are experiencing the power of God's Word for themselves.

The running water in Ezekiel's vision does three things.

It irrigates

The river from Ezekiel's temple irrigates the territory it crosses (v.7), enabling it to bear a range of crops and fruit normally impossible to grow in the Judean uplands except by irrigation.

The lesson for us? We cannot produce the `fruits of the Spirit' unless our lives are regularly watered by the Word of God. `Everything will live where the water goes' (v.9).

It oxygenates

When the river of Ezekiel's vision eventually enters the Dead Sea it does so in such volume and with such force that it dilutes the saltiness to such an extent that the saline waters turn fresh! As a result the Dead Sea (so called because of its lack of marine life) becomes the Living Sea, teeming with fish.

Surely the lesson here is that we need the Word of God to keeps us fresh! It's all too easy for our spirituality to get stale. It is as we open ourselves to the Word that we will be able to maintain our spiritual and corporate vitality. The Bible is one of the greatest agents of change in the world! It stimulates new ideas and new ways of thinking!

It generates

Implicit in the parabolic vision is the power of the river as it plunges down the wadis on the western slopes of the Jordan valley. Throughout that region, flash floods in the rainy season can be devastating, as Jesus' parable of the two houses illustrates - look what happened to the house built on sand (Matthew 7.24-27). And there are many modern examples of water generating electricity which make the same point, albeit more positively and contemporaneously.

So the lesson here is that giving God's Word its due place in Christian work makes that work effective. Jesus saw the Word of God as the seed which establishes God's kingdom in human society. If this is so, can anything be more powerful?

So as we prepare for the World Assembly, let us pray that the river of life may, indeed, flow through Midrand in October, imparting new life, fresh thinking and spiritual power not only to the 350 participants, but to our entire UBS family!

The vivid description of Ezekiel's progressive discovery of the volume of water as he followed the river from its source is a parable in itself! The water began as a trickle. 500 metres further on it reached Ezekiel's ankles; another 500 metres and it was knee-deep; a further 500 metres and it up to the waist.

By the time Ezekiel had walked 2,000 metres, it was deep enough to swim in (Ezekiel 47.3-5). What a picture of the increasing potential of God's Word as it is animated by his Spirit!

October 2000   GOING FOR GOLD

As I write, the Olympics are in full swing and across the globe, people are visiting Sydney every day (and night!) via television. The eyes of millions are glued to the small screen, fascinated by outstanding feats which push out the frontiers of the human body's performance further than they have ever been before.

The coveted prize of every contestant is to win `a gold'. To become an Olympic gold medallist is like standing on the summit of Mount Everest – you cannot go any higher!

`Going for gold' is the theme of an extensive program of Christian outreach being undertaken in Sydney and around the world to mark the Olympics. In this case, the `gold' in view is not a medal but a message (see Psalm 19.10)! At the heart of the Sydney outreach are the strikingly attractive Scripture materials produced by the Bible Society in Australia, which are being distributed to the many millions of visitors.

If I write this against the background of the Olympics, you may well read it against the background of the UBS World Assembly in Midrand, South Africa, 10-14 October. The Assembly will take place within a few hundred miles of the most famous gold mines in all the world. In Midrand in October, as in Sydney in September, we shall be `going for gold'. We shall seek the most effective strategic dirfection to take the UBS forward, and which will provide the world with that precious commodity which the psalmist describes as `more desirable than the finest gold'.

In the light of the outreach in Sydney and the consultation and discussions in Midrand, I want to share with you some endorsements of the Scriptures gleaned from previous centuries. As you read them, pray. Pray that the decisions of Midrand may lead to many millions of people in the 21st century discovering the Word of God, as so many have done in previous centuries.

Here is what some people have said about the Bible.

4th century

As in paradise, God walks in the Holy Scriptures seeking man.'
Divine Scripture is the feast of wisdom, and the single books are the various dishes.'

Ambrose

16th century

The Bible is alive, it speaks to me; it has feet, it runs after me; it has hands, it lays hold on me.'

Martin Luther

The Bible is the sceptre by which the heavenly King rules his Church.'

John Calvin

18th century

The Bible is an inexhaustible fountain of all truths. The existence of the Bible is the greatest blessing which humanity ever experienced.'

Immanuel Kant

I began not only to read, but to study the Bible as the only standard of truth, and the only model of pure religion.'

John Wesley

19th century

Most people are bothered by those passages in Scripture which they cannot understand; but as for me, I always noticed that the passages in Scripture which trouble me most are those that I do understand.'

Mark Twain

All that I am I owe to Jesus Christ revealed to me in the divine book.'

David Livingstone

20th century

The Bible that is falling apart usually belongs to someone who isn't.'

Vance Havner

Every Christian must refer always and everywhere to the Scriptures for all his choices, becoming like a child before it, seeking in it the most effective remedy against all his various weaknesses, and not daring to take a step without being illuminated by the divine ray of those words.'

Pope John Paul II

There are many books which I could read, but this is the only book which reads me.'

Tanzanian woman

`The wealth of manuscripts, and above all the narrow interval of time between the writing and the earliest extant copies, make it by far the best attested text of any ancient writing in the world.'

John Robinson, *Can We Trust the New Testament?*

`Lay hold on the Bible until the Bible lays hold of you.'

W H Houghton

`What makes the difference is not how many times you have been through the Bible, but how many times and how thoroughly the Bble has been through you.'

`Gipsy' Smith

Finally, let me share with you one more endorsement of the Bible. It comes from a former president of the United States of America:

`If a man is not familiar with the Bible, he has suffered a loss which he had better make all possible haste to correct.'

Theodore Roosevelt

None of us in the Bible Society family can forget that many people in today's world are unfamiliar with the Bible because of its scarcity rather than their lethargy. There's a lot of people out there still waiting for gold!

November 2000   **RECONCILIATION**

From now on, therefore, we regard no one from a human point of view; even though we once knew Christ from a human point of view, we know him no longer in that way. So if anyone is in Christ, there is a new creation: everything old has passed away; see everything has become new! All this is from God, who reconciled us to himself through Christ, and has given us the ministry of reconciliation.   (2 Corinthians 5.16-18, NRSV)

The Christian ministry of reconciliation - which the GNB translates as `the task of making others his [God's] friends also' - came unexpectedly to the surface no less than three times during the World Assembly in Midrand, South Africa, last month. Each of these unforeseen episodes dramatically illustrated for me Christian reconciliation transcending human barriers, and I want to share them with the wider UBS Fellowship.

Indian sub-continent

The first episode came on the Tuesday night. The focus of the closing worship for the day was on Asia. Liz Pass, our worship leader during the Assembly, chose three hymns from that region of the world and invited people present from each hymn's country of origin to come up on the stage and sing it with her and Impulse, the excellent African choir assisting her. So when she announced an Indian hymn, Bidyut Pramanik, General Secretary of the BSI, went forward on to the stage. When he got there he explained that he didn't know the hymn. Then Bishop Alexander Malik and Antony Lamuel of the Bible of Pakistan, called out from the congregation: 'We know that hymn in Pakistan.' Jokingly they added: 'And India is part of Pakistan!' They were immediately invited on to the stage and the three sang the hymn together and led the assembly in singing it. The hymn over, all three shook hands before returning to their seats.

Middle East

The second incident came on Thursday morning. We had heard only the day before of the outbreak of the Intifada in Israel and Palestine. Robert Cunville, Chair of the Bible Society of India, was due to lead the main prayer in the worship period which began the day. Half way through his prayer, Robert invited Doron Even Ari from Israel and Labib Madanat from Palestine to join him on the platform. Then he placed them one on either side, put his arms around them, and prayed very movingly for peace and reconciliation in the Holy Land. Beforehand I had offered Labib and Doron that I would request that no photographs be taken, in case this would make problems for them should any photograph reach the media. But both replied almost in unison: 'Photographs are OK. We want to stand up for what we believe'.

South Africa

The third incident was on the South Africa Night [Friday] - which, incidentally, was a tremendous success with top South African musicians providing very high calibre African music. Over 550 attended the event - in addition to World Assembly participants, large numbers of Bible Society of South Africa donors were present. [BSSA ran the evening in part as a fundraising event]. Guest of honour was Archbishop Desmond Tutu. He spoke at the beginning, referring in his remarks to the struggle against apartheid. Then he said grace in three languages - English, Afrikaans and Khosa. By praying in what was afterwards described to me as 'beautiful Afrikaans', Desmond Tutu was extending the

81

hand of friendship to Afrikaaners in the audience and underlining his commitment to reconciliation in the rainbow nation.

During the Assembly many participants referred to the sense of common purpose and unity which ran through our sessions in Midrand. Even when differences of opinion were expressed, these tended to enhance, rather than erode, our underlying sense of oneness simply because they were seen as reflecting diversity rather than disunity. And these three unforeseen incidents - from the Indian sub-continent, the Middle East and South Africa - confirm that our Bible Society family, in addition to achieving in large measure reconciliation within our Fellowship, is also promoting reconciliation in the outside world.

December 2000   MAGNIFICAT

We are now in the season of Advent when churches all over the world celebrate the incarnation. So this month I'd like to begin by focussing on the greatest song of Advent celebration ever written - the *Magnificat* of the Virgin Mary.

The traditional title of this famous hymn - which is found in Luke 1.46-55 - is taken from its first word in the Vulgate [Latin] version: *Magnificat anima mea Dominum*, meaning literally `My soul magnifies the Lord'. This opening stanza stresses that Advent is a time to rejoice! Here is how the CEV renders Luke 1.46,47:

With all my heart I praise the Lord,
and I am glad because of God my Saviour.

In many cultures the run up to Christmas is an exceedingly busy time. It's the period when many retail outlets in the western world achieve the largest proportion of their sales. And Bible Societies probably distribute more Scripture selections during Advent than at any other time. Of course, such `busyness' is not inappropriate. But let us ensure that it does not deprive us of the energy or the time to *rejoice* in the miracle of Bethlehem!

Assuming that we can preserve the human energy and create the time to celebrate in depth the mystery of the incarnation of the Son of God, how might we go about doing so? We find the answers in Mary's Song of Praise! There's so much here to inspire us. But for now I would like to underline just three emphases in this song.

God's holy name

God All-Powerful has done great things for me,
and his name is holy.   (v.49, CEV)

When the Bible says that God is holy it means that he is set apart from us, exalted, transcendent. Isaiah's description of his awesome vision of the Lord in the temple (Isaiah 6.1-5) bears this out.

The reminder that God's name is holy provides the prompt we need in a world informed by secularised media to realise that God's presence in Bethlehem is transcendent as well as immanent. The halo surrounding the head of the Christ child on Christmas cards suggests that Advent is a season in which, like Moses before the bush, we are on holy ground. For Bethlehem is the place where God came decisively into the world for our salvation.

If Christmas is for us only a common place festival, we miss the point! We truly celebrate Christmas when we rejoice in the coming of God our Saviour! And our rejoicing, like Mary's, will focus on the mystery of the Son of God becoming a human being.

> In Christianity everything that has to do with the 'way' is concentrated in a Person. The way to God is not primarily a psychological process. It is not a geographical route; nor a religious hierarchy; nor a holy shrine; nor esoteric knowledge. The Christian way to God is a person who becomes the object of that belief and commitment which is called faith. In Jesus Christ God and man meet.
>
> - John A Mackay, *A Preface to Christian Theology*, p.70f

God's mighty power

God has used his powerful arm
to scatter those who are proud.
He drags strong rulers from their thrones
and puts humble people in places of power.
God gives the hungry good things to eat,
and sends the rich away with nothing.   (vv.51-53, CEV)

Mary reflects on the way God intervenes against the proud and the powerful, siding with the humble and the hungry. She anticipates that the incarnation will express solidarity with the latter and be seen as a threat by the former.

This is why our Christmas celebration, if it is real, will mean helping the poor and feeding the hungry. Although the lavish the self-indulgence of the modern western Christmas seems to deny it, Christmas is primarily for the poor. Martin Luther King's testimony in this regard will help us to focus biblically this Advent:

> Despite the fact that all too often people see the church a power opposed to any change, in fact, the church preserves a powerful ideal which urges people toward the summits and opens their eyes as to their own destiny. From the hot spots of Africa to the black areas of Alabama, I have seen men and women rising and shaking off their chains. They had just discovered they were God's children, and that, as God's children, it was impossible to enslave them.

Given the bitter ethno-religious conflict raging in the Holy Land, it will be particularly appropriate this year for us all to celebrate Christmas by doing all we can where we are to establish justice, to demonstrate compassion and to promote reconciliation.

God's perpetual mercy

He always shows mercy
to everyone who worships him. (v.50, CEV)

He helps his servant Israel
and is always merciful to his people.
The Lord made this promise to our ancestors,
to Abraham and his family forever! (vv.54,55, CEV)

The incarnation, together with the cross and the resurrection, constitute the bedrock of the Good News that God so loved the world that he gave his only Son. The birth of Jesus not only expressed divine solidarity with us members of the human race; it also brought a Saviour to us! And the salvation which this Saviour has brought us is summed up in words like `mercy' and `love'.

We see the love of God more clearly at Bethlehem and Calvary than anywhere else in the universe! Every Christmas and Easter, as we celebrate these foundational events, we have an opportunity to sense the heart of God beating for our world.

Henri Nouwen tells how intensely moving he found Rembrandt's famous painting of the father of the returned prodigal clasping to his breast the head of his kneeling son. Reflecting on his vocation as a priest, Nouwen wrote:

> I have to kneel before the Father, put my ear against his heart and listen without interruption, to the heartbeat of God. Then, and only then, can I say carefully and very gently what I hear. I know now that I have to speak from eternity into time, from the lasting joy into the

passing realities of our short existence in this world, from the house of love into houses of fear, from God's abode into the dwellings of human beings.

- *The Return of the Prodigal Son: A Story of Homecoming* (p.17)

Just as the painting powerfully reinforced the words of the parable for Nouwen, Christmas as one of the symbols of our faith can fortify our commitment in Bible work to demonstrate and communicate the love of God to a lost and fractured world.

Celebrating Christmas repeatedly year on year reminds us that God's mercy flows towards us in wave after wave! It tells us that his mercies towards us are piled so high they reach the heavens. May Christmas this year be no exception!

A final thought on Christmas from Ronald Knox:

To us Christians, the first Christmas Day is the solstice or bottleneck of history. Things got worse till then, ever since we had lost paradise; things are to get better since then, till we reach paradise once more. History is shaped like an X.

January 2001   **TOGETHER**

As we begin 2001 - which many people believe is the first year of the Third Millennium - it is surely appropriate for us to renew our commitment to our common task in the Bible cause.

Last October this common task was defined with fresh clarity by the Midrand Assembly as:

Achieving the widest possible, effective and meaningful distribution of the Holy Scriptures

- in languages and media which meet the needs of people world wide,

- in translations that are faithful to the Scripture texts in their original languages and which communicate the biblical message

- at prices people can afford,

and of helping people interact with the Word of God.

You will find among the Midrand Assembly papers enclosed with this mailing the longer document entitled *The Identity and Ethos of the United Bible Societies* from which this purpose statement is taken.

Midrand delegates made a public commitment in the closing session to achieve this common task through the grace of our Lord Jesus Christ. While they did that on behalf of the Bible Societies they represented, those present constituted only a small number of the thousands of active members of the Bible Society family. So it would be good if *all* of us were to renew that commitment by making it our own. And surely there's no better time to do so than at the beginning of a new year!

There are at least three reasons why we should!

A sacred task

First, because our common task is *sacred*. The psalmist in giving thanks to the Lord for his steadfast love and faithfulness makes a remarkable affirmation of the sacredness of God's Word by closely associating it with the Lord's name: 'You have exalted your name and your word above everything' (Psalm 138.2 NRSV). The reference here may be to God's Word as promise (cf. Ps 18.30; 119.38,50,140), and the CEV helpfully translates the verse as 'You were true to your word and made yourself more famous than ever before.'

The sacredness of God's Word is also underlined by Jesus when he identified it with the seed of the Kingdom of heaven. That kingdom (or kingship) is established on earth - in individual lives and in community values - as the Word of God is translated into new languages and media, produced in print and non-print formats, distributed in churches and in public arenas, and received in life-changing encounters with the biblical text. It is as people personally receive and believe God's Word that his kingship is acknowledged on earth.

All this underlines just how special it is to be involved in Bible work. There is no other work closer to the heart of God, and no other activity nearer the centre of God's purposes for the world.

A secular task

Second, our common task is *secular*! God wants us to give his Word to the secular order as well as to the church!

Just as in the beginning God's powerful words called the universe into existence as a cosmos, an organised system (Genesis 1; cf Psalm 33.6; Hebrews 11.3), so it sustains today the complex systems of galaxies and ecosystems which attract the attention and excite the fascination of the world's scientists. God's Word to the creation is obviously prior to the formation of the earliest Scriptures, but it resonates with his Word to us through the prophets and apostles.

Our task is secular not simply because the Word we translate and distribute holds the secret of the universe. It is secular also because this same Word contains a blueprint for human society. It tells us that humans are made in the image of God (Genesis 1.26,27), creating a correspondence between us and God. Just as an image in a mirror subsists in reflection from the original, so we are created in a basic structure of dependence on God and for communion with God. We are truly ourselves when we respond to God, answering the word of him in whose image we are created.

This is why we:

- market the Scriptures in the public square
- commend the Bible to politicians, business people and other public figures
- encourage the media to incorporate biblical values in the world views they communicate.

We do this because we believe that the Scriptures can make the world a better place.

A strategic task

Third, our common task is *strategic*. The work of the Bible Societies not only accelerates the coming of the Kingdom of God. It not only makes the world a better place. It also facilitates the unity of the Church.

In many countries the Bible Societies fulfill a unique catalytic role in bringing the churches together in fulfilling their mission to announce the Good News of Jesus Christ. The lack of visible unity among the churches has been described as a scandal. But it's not a disaster! For there is much common ground that all churches recognise and affirm, not least the authority of Holy Scripture. Because of the centrality of the Bible our programs to translate and distribute the Scriptures tend to attract a broader range of inter-church and inter-confessional cooperation than is the case in most (if not all) other inter-church activities.

In this way Bible Societies fulfill a key role in helping to heal the fractured body of Christ. At a time when the ecumenical movement is losing popular support, when new churches are arising with little enthusiasm for mainline churches, and when confessional boundaries seem to be hardening, we in the Bible Society movement have an enormous opportunity - and responsibility - to enable Christians who differ on confessional matters to work together in the service of the Word of God.

The strategic importance of this role cannot be over-emphasised. For manifesting the unity of the body of Christ is mission critical to the churches.

Remember how our Lord prayed for all who would believe in him. 'Father! May they be in us, just as you are in me and I am in you. May they be one, so that the world may believe that you sent me.' (John 17.20,21, GNB).

That's why before God we should celebrate our common task at the beginning of this New Year. We need to rejoice more than we are inclined to do in the fact that, in fulfilling our calling, we - the UBS family - help the Kingdom of God to come, we strengthen society and we challenge the churches to move closer towards that unity which, when demonstrated, will persuade the world to believe in Jesus Christ.

I invite you all to celebrate this unique ministry during your first Bible Society Board meeting of 2001 in whatever way you feel appropriate, inviting Board members and staff alike to renew their commitment to this great task in the months and years ahead.

Finally, there is one more aspect of our common task which is important to remember at the beginning of a new century. It will be *successful*! The prophet Isaiah assures us that God's words will never return without doing all that he sends them to do (Isaiah 55.10-11). So take courage! God's Word will not fail us, it will not fail the churches and it will not fail the world!

YEAR FOUR

ETHOS

The *Golden Rule* (`Do unto others as you would have them do unto you') is recognised by the major religions. Judaism, Christianity and Islam are committed to it because, as Jesus tells us, it is what the Scriptures of the Old Testament are all about (Matthew 7.12). In addition, it is found, albeit in negative form, in Hinduism, Buddhism and Confucianism, and is also reflected in modern Humanism.

This almost universal respect for the Golden Rule reflects a widespread recognition of the importance of human relationships. Agreements can be signed, joint ventures initiated and networks established, but all of us acknowledge that they will come to nothing unless the personal relationships among those who seek to make them work are founded and built on trust and transparency.

Alas! Widespread respect for the Golden Rule does not mean it is universally practised. Far from it! The first year of the Third Millennium witnessed a series of conflicts (in the Balkans, the Holy Lands, Sudan, Nigeria, Kashmir, Indonesia, etc.) operating under the *Iron Rule* (`Do it to others before they do it to you'). In addition to these tragic conflicts, there are many ethnic and religious tensions and divisions arising from observance of the *Silver Rule* (`Love those who love you' with its corollary `Hate those who hate you').

On a brighter note, the customer service revolution of the 1970s and 1980s in the business world, which saw companies moving from selling what they produced to producing what others want to buy, led an American management guru[1] to articulate the *Platinum Rule* [`Treat others as others would have you treat them'].

Higher still

A close study of the Gospels makes it clear that Jesus goes higher still. Jesus urges us to treat others as he has treated us. He denies the Iron Rule, goes beyond than the Silver Rule, further than the Golden Rule and higher even

---

[1] Tony Alessandra in *The Platinum Rule: Discover the Four Basic Business Personalities - and How they Can Lead You to Success*, [1996], by Tony Alessandra and Michael J O'Connor.

than the Platinum Rule! Jesus' memorable and demanding saying `Love one another as I have loved you' (John 13.34f. NRSV) is described as the *Titanium Rule* by Leonard Sweet, a contemporary American evangelical thinker.

This is radical stuff! Jesus is saying that we are truly human and really free when we show love, understanding and forgiveness to others. How different from the prevailing ethos in so many societies where self-interest, bitter antagonism and even physical violence are all too common! The sad fact is that in so many areas we are today losing our humanness. David Smith, Co-Director of the Whitefield Institute in Oxford, England, makes the telling point in his recent book *Crying in the Wilderness: Evangelism and Mission in Today's Culture* that, while the 19th century ended with growing numbers of people finding it difficult to believe in God, the problem at the end of the 20th century was how to continue to believe in man.

True human-ness

In this situation Christians are called to demonstrate true human-ness in their relationships. Every local church, every Christian organisation, every Bible Society has the God-given task to demonstrate - both in its internal relationships and in its public relations - the plausibility of the claim that following Jesus Christ makes the world a better place.

UBS President Samuel Escobar reminded as at the World Assembly that we are called `to walk in the light'. He was quoting from 1 John, a letter which bluntly states that `if we are walking in darkness, we lie and do not do what is true' (1 John 1.6). That same letter defines walking in darkness as hating others (1 John 2.11, NRSV), and Dr Escobar rightly went on to challenge all of us to ensure we have `a firm commitment to be sure that the way in which the Bible Societies do their business does not contradict the teaching of God's Word about human behavior'.

`I love, therefore I am'

`I think, therefore, I am' was the identity statement of the enlightenment era. Today in the consumer society this has been replaced by `I shop, therefore, I am' as the preferred index of human identity. But in the counter culture, which the church [and hopefully also the UBS] is called upon to become, the indicator of true humanity can only be `I love, therefore, I am'. For `whoever loves a brother or sister lives in the light, and in such a person there is no cause for stumbling'. (1 John 2.10, NRSV)

This must mean that our identity is found in community, and not in isolation. William Tyndale, the great English translator of the Bible, first noticed that the word *myself* does not appear in the English Bible. Leonard Sweet suggests that what Tyndale meant is that no individual `I' can become `myself' without `you' and `others'.

It would be worthwhile for each of us to pause for a moment and reflect on how we interact with one another as staff, Board members, UBS colleagues. Do we follow the Titanium standard or the Platinum? The Gold or the Silver? Or - dread the thought! - the Iron?

Stephen Covey, the American management guru, relates *ethos* to *pathos*. He tells us the ancient Greeks used ethos to describe personal integrity and credibility, while pathos for them was essentially feeling. Both formed a counter-balance to *logos*, the reasoning logical approach. Interacting with and submitting to the text of Scripture enables us to develop a spiritual pathos in our corporate culture which will make our ethos attractive and our logos convincing.

Finally, two quotations to help us remember that we need one another.
`Holy ground is never private turf, but always communal space.'
-Kenda Creasy and Ron Foster
`I am because we are.'
- Khosa proverb, South Africa.

March 2001   GLOBAL FELLOWSHIP

St Paul begins his First Letter to the Corinthians by underlining that the `Church of God that is in Corinth' was intimately related to `all those who in every place call on the name of our Lord Jesus Christ' (1Corinthians 1.2, NRSV).

The Christian Church can be both local and global because it is essentially a fellowship: `God is faithful; by him you were called into the fellowship (*koinonia*) of his Son, Jesus Christ our Lord.' (1.9, RSV). In his book *Ecumenics: The Science of the Church Universal,* John A Mackay – a former President of Princeton Seminary - points out that `The early Christian community was a *koinonia*, a fellowship, before it was an *ecclesia*, or assembly.'

This New Testament concept of *koinonia* is fundamental, not only to the identity of the Church, but also to church-related organisations like UBS. The basic assumption of the Midrand statement on *The Identity and Ethos of the United Bible Societies* is that we are `a world fellowship'.

This may be an appropriate time to pause and reflect on what it means to be a `world fellowship', because we are in the midst of changing to the new governance structure approved at Midrand. At the beginning of this month the four new Area Boards met for the first time. And this month and next the elections to the new Global Board are taking place. If, indeed, the Church was a *koinonia* before it was an *ecclesia*, surely the lesson for us in the Bible Societies - which are intimately related to the churches - is that successful UBS structures will depend on our being a healthy UBS fellowship.

The word `fellowship' was, and is, also used of secular and non-Christian bodies. But there it tends to describe men and women united by common aspirations, while in its Christian usage it refers to disparate people united by a common experience of the love of God.

Mackay in his *Ecumenics* distinguishes Christian fellowship from what he calls `Star friendship' and `Tavern friendship'. The concept of Star friendship is borrowed from the German philosopher Friedrich Nietzsche, to describe the correct observance of protocol. In this protocol pattern of friendship, `friends' are like the planets orbiting the sun with only a deferential nod to one another as they pass in the coldness of space. This `Star friendship' is correct, but cold.

`Tavern friendship,' on the other hand, is a phrase Mackay borrows from the Hispanic world to describe the happy encounter of a party. People have a good time together, but never come to know one another deeply, or become relevant to one another's needs. There is a lot of joviality, but no intimacy and no personal encounter.

I don't wish to suggest that Christian fellowship does not involve observing correct protocol or jovial partying. Far from it! I simply want to make the point that Christian fellowship is so much more! It involves mutual reverence for one another and a commitment to a deep sense of togetherness. In this fellowship each friend continues to be part of the other's life and concern, and accepts that the fulfilment of responsibility is more basic than the insistence on rights. Service takes precedence over benefits.

The challenge we face at the beginning of a new chapter in UBS history is to ensure that such true Christian fellowship is incarnated in our corporate life at all levels – local, regional, area, and global. The UBS is a *world* fellowship of Bible Societies simply because it embraces the whole world and serves all the churches. But it can be a world *fellowship* only insofar as we allow God to reproduce in us and through us some of the key attributes of *koinonia* which we encounter in the Acts of the Apostles and in the Letters of the New Testament.

While there are aspects of *koinonia* which apply exclusively to the churches, there are others which apply to all networks engaged in Christian mission. I want to highlight three attributes of koinonia which, I suggest, ought to be vital components of our UBS ethos. These can be summed up in three graphic images. The first is the Fish.

A Fellowship of the Fish

Because the letters of the Greek word for fish (*ichthus*) form the initial letters of the words making up the phrase 'Jesus Christ God and Saviour', the early Christians made the symbol of the fish their sign of identity under persecution. This sign, which today is found on a range of Christian literature from letterheads to bumper stickers, was first inscribed on the walls of the catacombs of Rome where first century Christians met in secret to worship.

These early Christian believers were a disparate bunch! Socially they were made up of slaves and free citizens. Ethnically they were Romans, Jews, Greeks and `barbarians'. The only thing this heterogeneous group had in common was their allegiance to Jesus Christ! But that common allegiance had become the most powerful influence in their lives, and bound them together in a world which worked hard to pull them apart.

The most acute tension in the early Church was between Jewish and Gentile believers. In a sense it foreshadowed the tensions which today exist between Catholics and Evangelicals in Latin America, between Orthodox and Baptists in Russia, and between traditional and radical (Pentecostal) Protestants within the Protestant confession. In the Bible Society movement we experience all of these tensions. If we didn't we would not be faithfully serving all the churches! And we don't have the luxury of being able to pick and choose the churches we work with, for as *The Identity and Ethos of the United Bible Society* says, 'The Bible Societies seek to carry out their task in partnership and cooperation with all Christian churches and with church related organisations.'

The key to our serving successfully disparate church groupings is to encourage them to fix their eyes on the sign of the Fish! For even the most disparate Christian churches can engage together in Bible work as they focus on their primary (Christian) identity before their secondary (confessional) identity. This is not to suggest that our secondary identities are unimportant. On the contrary, I believe they must be respected. But they must be seen in the perspective of St Paul that `Christ is the only foundation' (1 Corinthians 3.11, CEV).

It is because the UBS is a fellowship of the Fish that we are called to live in the midst of the tensions, but above the rivalries, of the ecumenical scene, and affirm that we are a world fellowship which transcends race, culture, nationality, ideology and ecclesiastical affiliation!

A Fellowship of the Towel

Jesus taught his disciples to care for one another.

This is markedly brought out in the passage describing him washing their feet. Interestingly it was precisely at a time when he was acutely aware that 'the Father had given all things into his hands' that he chose to assume the role of the servant of his disciples. 'Jesus knew he had come from God and would go back to God. He also knew that the Father had given him complete power. So during the meal Jesus got up, removed his outer garment, and wrapped a towel around his waist. He put some water in a large bowl. Then he began washing his disciples' feet and drying them with the towel he was wearing.' (John 13.3-5, CEV)

So it is not surprising that the early Church sometimes used the word *koinonia* in the sense of practical sharing with those who are less fortunate. A case in point is St Paul's use of the term to describe the collection he took from his churches for the relief of poor famine-stricken Christians in Jerusalem and Judea (Romans 15.26; 2 Corinthians 8.4; 9.13).

It is, therefore, manifestly consistent with both the example of Jesus and the practice of the early Church for *The Identity and Ethos of the United Bible Societies* to say: 'The Bible Societies are an expression of the fellowship of God's people sharing their resources. These include, for example, spiritual gifts, knowledge, money, time, talents and technology.'

Such sharing will involve serving one another. This doesn't mean that one Bible Society does all the serving and another is being perpetually served. Rather it means that both are given an opportunity to serve one another. It's relatively easy to find ways in which the strong can serve the weak. It's more difficult to discover how the weak can serve the strong. Yet, I believe we must find imaginative ways to do this if we wish to avoid falling into a patron-client model. We need to find new ways of exhibiting partnership (one of the meanings of *koinonia* in the New Testament), and avoiding patronage.

As a fellowship of the Towel our vocation is to encourage and enable mutual service.

A Fellowship of the Road

The earliest name for what later became known as Christianity was 'the Way' (Acts 9.2). The early Church was seen both from within and from without as a community on the march! It rapidly spread from Jerusalem to Judea and

Samaria and then to Antioch. From Antioch it was taken to Cyprus and to Turkey and then to Greece. Before the New Testament closes it had reached Rome, Egypt and North Africa, Illyricum and possibly also Spain.

The Bible Societies are among those who have inherited this tradition of mission to the world. *The Identity and Ethos of the United Bible Societies* defines our common task as:

`achieving the widest possible, effective and meaningful distribution of the Holy Scriptures
- in languages and media which meet the needs of people world wide,
- in translations that are faithful to the Scripture texts in their original languages, and which communicate the biblical message
- at prices people can afford
and of helping people interact with the Word of God.'

And the rationale of our long history of cooperation is explained as follows: `Coming from different backgrounds and possessing a variety of spiritual gifts they [Bible Societies] have envisioned and empowered one another to further their work together.'

The great object of working together is more quickly and more effectively to fulfil our mission of helping the churches provide every person with an opportunity – and, if necessary, repeated opportunities – to receive the Holy Scriptures and thus to face the claims of Jesus Christ.

That is why the UBS must always remain a fellowship of the Road! For we are called to carry the Holy Scriptures, not only to the churches, but also with the churches, along the highways and byways of the secular world.

And it is precisely because we are a fellowship of the Road that we need to measure our performance, to discover our ROM (return on mission). Otherwise we could be very active, but very ineffective! We need to ask this question of every Bible Society and UBS activity: Is it carrying the churches further along the road which leads to that great day when the people will bring the glory and the honour of the nations of the world into the New Jerusalem (Revelation 21.26)?

Both the Old and the New Testaments regard the people of God as pilgrims on an unfinished journey. And the story of that journey is the framework of the Bible from Genesis to Revelation, from Adam and Eve to the New Jerusalem. That journey is not yet over! So Bible Societies are participants in the biblical story, not mere spectators of it! Our task is to help the churches and humanity to complete the journey and thus to help the story unfold and move it towards its consummation. It is for this reason that we are a fellowship of the Road!

Finally, one further quotation from John A Mackay:

> The Christian Church as a Fellowship of the Road, a Community on the march, expresses the inmost nature and genius of the Church in the context of the Bible. This is, moreover, the image of the Church which is most relevant to the present human situation and which offers the greatest challenge to Christian thought and imagination.
>
> *- Ecumenics: The Science of the Church Universal* (p.92)

April 2001   EASTER WORK

Sometimes in Bible work we can get discouraged.

- The need is so great, but the resources aren't enough!
- In some countries upwards of 50 people eagerly share one Bible; in others many homes have an abundance of copies, few of which are read.
- We work long hours and constantly feel the pressure of deadlines.
- We worry that the focus is too often on quantity - not quality – Scripture distribution. We are haunted by the Psalmist's assertion: `Unless the Lord builds the house, those who build it labour in vain.'

If we resonate with any of these sentiments, Easter is good news for us! For Easter provides a spiritual context to our work as well as bringing joy to our faith. Listen to what St Paul says! He ends his great exposition of the Resurrection with these words:

`Therefore, my beloved, be stedfast, immovable, always excelling in the work of the Lord, because you know that in the Lord your labour is not in vain.' (1 Corinthians 15.58, NRSV)

The Greek word *kenos* (`in vain') in this verse is variously rendered in the English versions. Here are some examples:

- `You know that nothing you do in the Lord's service is ever *useless*.' (GNB)
- `Be sure that nothing you do for him is ever *lost* or ever *wasted*.' (J B Phillips)
- `You may be sure that in the Lord your labour is never *thrown away*.' (Moffat)

What a message of encouragement when we are downcast!

If we take a closer look at 1 Corinthians 15, and, as it were, look out on our work through the open door way of the empty tomb, we discover three things that the message of Easter brings to our work.

Perspective

The first is perspective. Go back to 1 Corinthians 15.58. Note the relationship between `the work of the Lord' and our `labour' (`service', GNB) in it. Our service will not be `in vain' because it is, in fact, part of the work of the Lord who will achieve the resurrection of the dead. If he will achieve that, surely he will make our lowly service for him fruitful and worthwhile! And, taking 1 Corinthians 15 as a whole, we see that our work is not only a prelude to our resurrection; it is also the sequel to Christ's resurrection! For, `if Christ has not been raised, your faith is futile' (15.17, NRSV). The panorama stretching from the resurrection of Jesus around 30 AD to the resurrection of the dead at the end of the age is the background against which we are to view our involvement in the work of the Lord in our generation.

Your service in the Bible Society movement is a vital part of this cosmic work of the Lord! You are servicing the communication system of the Kingdom of God!

Potential

The second is potential. Christian work has a potential far above normal. The Hebrew word rendered in the NRSV by the expression `in vain' in Psalm 127.1 (`labour in vain') is translated `worthless' in Psalms 60.11 and 108.12. These last two references have a military context, and the phrase common to both psalms `human help is worthless' is uttered as the reason why divine help against the enemy is needed. The CEV translates both verses as follows:

Help us defeat our enemies!
No one else can rescue us.'

Easter is a reminder that the help available to us is so much greater than human resources! The Word which we translate and distribute announces the good news that `God, in his great mercy, gave us new life by raising Jesus Christ from death.' (1Peter 1.3, GNB) And it is through the communication of this good news that the new life flowing from the resurrection of Jesus continues to touch and transform human lives today.

Never doubt that your service in the Bible cause has enormous potential! It enables others to receive the most powerful life-transforming message in the world. What you do has the potential to change lives, impact communities and change the course of history!

This is being written from New York. I am here to attend the annual meeting of the Forum of Bible Agencies which this year is the guest of the American Bible Society. The Forum is a network of almost 20 agencies committed to the translation and/or distribution of the Holy Scriptures which meets annually to encourage cooperation.

New York looks splendid in the beautiful spring weather. The trees in Central Park are bursting into leaf, the cherry trees lining the avenues are in blossom, and the clear blue skies are showing off the famous Manhattan skyline at its best.

Our meetings – attended by over 40 people - are turning out to be inspiring as well as informative. More about this in a moment.

First, let me tell you of a visit I made to the Barnes and Noble bookstore on Broadway, a few blocks north of the ABS building. I walked there one afternoon to obtain *The Prayer of Jabez*, a little book currently topping the sales charts on this side of the Atlantic. According to the New York best sellers' list, 4 million copies were sold last year, and half a million in the first three months of this year. A simple little book about prayer by Bruce Wilkinson, founder and president of Walk Thru the Bible Ministries – written in simple, racy language employing lots of memorable `one-liners' - it is striking a chord among many North American professionals

Here are some examples:

- Jabez is found `hiding in the least-read section of one of the least-read books of the Bible.'
- `Living large for God'.
- Jabez is `the Bible's little big man' who `is remembered not for what he did, but for what he prayed.'
- `Under the surface [of Jabez' prayer] lies a giant paradigm breaker that runs exactly opposite to the way we think.'
- `Blessing is not about sneezing'.

Wilkinson quotes the prayer as follows:

And Jabez called on the God of Israel saying
`Oh, that you would bless me indeed,
and enlarge my territory,
that your hand would be with me,
and that you would keep me from evil,
that I may not cause pain!'
So God granted him what he requested.   (1 Chronicles 4.10, NKJV)

What has this to do with the Forum of Bible Agencies? Answer: The remarkable resonance between Bruce Wilkinson's commentary on this prayer and this year's agenda of the Forum!

`Hiding in ... one of the least-read books of the Bible'

The Forum heard that Bible use is dropping dramatically in some western countries. In the United States, for example, over the past 30 years the proportion of the population which rarely or never read the Bible has risen from 24% to 41%. The root of the problem is rising post-literacy as well as increased secularisation. We heard that a recent survey in Denmark reveals that 1 in 3 Danes normally do not read anything

One of the Forum's most stimulating sessions was a brainstorm on inductive Bble study, and how to focus group Bible study on impact as well as on analysis. The Scripture Gift Mission won the admiration of the group for its new Scripture portions and selections targeted at postmodern young people. The presenter was convinced that it *is* possible to get today's young consumers into the Word of God. And the need to multiply non-print media Scriptures came up again and again.

`Living large for God'

The Forum heard that prayers like `Oh, that you would enlarge my territory' are being misapplied in the North America, where market share is becoming all-consuming to the extent that some publishers publicly attack the Bible versions of their competitors. Sadly the impact of such negative advertising on the non-Bible reading public is to turn them off!

In contrast, the Forum members reaffirmed their commitment to be courteous and accurate when publishing comments about each other and never to refer negatively in public to a member agency. At the same time they were acutely conscious of the need to `think big' and `pray big' in order to extend translation and expand distribution so that we can catch up with God as he builds his Church today. Members expressed a willingness to go beyond sharing information to consider developing common strategies which will complement and reinforce each other's ministries.

`Blessing is not about sneezing'

In some western cultures when someone sneezes we say `Bless you!' Bruce Wilkinson comments: `No wonder the meaning of blessing gets watered down to something vague and innocuous like "Have a nice day." No wonder so many Christians aren't as desperate as Jabez was to receive it.'

This week the Forum is recognising that blessing on the Bible cause is ultimately not about translating, not about publishing, not about multiplying media and formats. Rather blessing in our context is about the Scriptures becoming 'words of power' in the life of those who hear, view or read them. It's about witnessing the Bible become a life-transforming book in the churches' worship services and in programs of evangelism. This week I think we have come to a common conviction that personal, small group and congregational engagement with the text of Scripture is vital if God's purpose for his Word is to be accomplished.

'A giant paradigm breaker'

'At first glance,' writes Wilkinson, 'the four requests [of Jabez] may strike you as sincere, sensible, even noble, but not terribly remarkable. Yet under the surface of each lies a giant paradigm breaker that runs exactly opposite to the way you and I usually think.' Prayer as a paradigm breaker!

In this year's meeting of the Forum I am conscious of a strong focus on prayer. Not only do we pray at the beginning of each day in the devotions. Several times the business has been suspended briefly and someone invited to pray for a specific item on the agenda or for someone undertaking a vital task. I have been thrilled by this corporate recognition that only if God's hand is with us – which Wilkinson describes as truly 'the touch of greatness' - will we be able to accomplish the task.

Returning to Wilkinson's *Prayer of Jabez* and the Forum meeting in the home of the American Bible Society, it's important to add one thing. It's this: despite the vivacious style of the former and the animated atmosphere of the latter, both book and forum are really very ordinary things. The book is slender and, indeed, it is simplistic. Yet it's having an extraordinary impact. The forum is composed of agencies which have been better at competing than at co-operating. Yet all over the world lives are being impacted. Why? Because today God is using the testimony of the book and the ministry of the Bible agencies. And when God's hand is upon us we can expect extraordinary things to happen!

June 2001 CREATING CORPORATE CULTURE

I want to begin this month by quoting from the Good News Translation – but not from the biblical text!

> Paul's Second Letter to Timothy *consists largely of personal advice to Timothy, as a younger colleague and assistant. The main theme is endurance. Timothy is advised and encouraged to keep on witnessing faithfully to Jesus Christ, to hold to the true teaching of the Good News and the Old Testament, and to do his duty as teacher and evangelist, all in the face of suffering and opposition.*

> - GNB Introduction to 2 Timothy

There is every reason why, as a fellowship of Bible Societies, we should view the entirety of our corporate life within a biblical frame, and not restrict the role of the Bible to our specifically religious activities such as daily or weekly prayer times and devotions held at the beginning of Board meetings.

There is certainly much in 2 Timothy which is relevant to what Bible Societies do! Timothy is told his task would be tough! This is seen very clearly in the opening verses of chapter 2, where Timothy is urged to `Be strong...' (v.1), and to be prepared to take his part in suffering (v.3).

In verses 3 to 7, three striking images are introduced to help Timothy better understand that his task calls for hard work. These are the images of *soldier*, *athlete*, and *farmer*. Each image is reinforced by the next - a good example of how to make a point effectively.

While all three have a common primary import, each has its own unique nuance, which, I believe, helps us understand better our task as national Bible Societies.

Soldier

The first image suggests the importance of *strategy*.

We are told that a soldier obeys his commanding officer. And we know that the commanding officer is ultimately responsible to a General. The Greek word for general is *strategos*, from which western languages get the term `strategy'.

What is strategy? A vast literature in management studies seeks to answer this. Answers are varied and not always consistent. But one of the most convincing is that the foundation of a strategy consists of being sure of three things:

1 Who you are
2 What you do
3 Where you want to go

It's fascinating that these three points resonate with what happened at the Midrand Assembly, for there the UBS laid a new foundation for strategy. In the *Identity and Ethos* document we affirmed *who we are* and *what we do*. And in the *Direction from Midrand* we agreed *where we want to go* in the next four years.

The Assembly came to closure on UBS identity, mission, and vision for 2000-4.

Vision has been defined as *imagining the future*. The world of sport demonstrates the power of imagining the future, for most successful athletes visualise success before achieving it. Let's look at two current examples!

Tiger Woods, the champion golfer was taught by his father, Earl, to form before each shot a mental image of the ball rolling into the hole.

Laura Wilkinson, the US Olympics high diver, only six months before the Sydney Olympics, broke her foot in three places while training. For the next three months Laura was unable to enter the water because of her cast, but she spent hours every day on the diving platform, visualising each of her dives. She was able to resume actual practice only weeks before the start of the Olympics. Yet, she pulled off a huge upset, winning the 10 metre dive gold medal!

Ian Robertson of Trinity College, Dublin, and author of *Mind Sculpture*, believes that 'Visualisation can literally reprogram the neural circuitry of the brain, directly improving performance.'

What is true in sport is also true in business and in Bible work! Indeed, it should be especially true for us, for visualisation of the future is an act of faith. And if our faith is focused on Jesus Christ and energised by the Holy Spirit, surely the natural power of visualisation to improve human performance will be greatly enhanced! While a realistic vision must pass the tests of desirability and feasibility, it is only as our Bible Societies imagine the future we desire to see in three to four years time, that we will be able to plan for it.

Thus vision leads to strategy – or ought to! Visualising success or imagining the future is not enough. *The future must be built as well as imagined.*

It is built by developing strategies and plans to implement the vision. The World Assembly can agree a 'strategic direction' (or 'vision') but it does not develop strategies to implement that direction. Implementation is primarily the task of the national Bible Societies, supported by the UBS Global and Area Boards and the UBS Service Centres. If the long-term objectives of the Midrand Direction are to be achieved, they will need to be translated and expanded into short term objectives which will be realised by designing and adopting specific strategies and plans. These strategies will focus on both *program* and *services*. Program plans are prepared by the Bible Societies; service plans by UBS service arms.

Eight months on from Midrand, many Bible Societies are evaluating how far they have got in implementation of the vision. This is a question the new Area Boards and Global Board have also begun to address, and I hope that by October – one year after the Assembly and on the eve of new UBS financial year – strategies and plans at national, regional and inter-regional levels will be updated to enable Bible work to advance on all fronts.

Athlete

Returning to the biblical frame in 2 Timothy 2.3-7, we come to the second image. While again the primary import is hard work, I want to suggest that for us the most significant nuance here is *energy*.

The idea of the athlete keeping to the rules in order to win the prize suggests discipline, training, concentration, and energy-building. Without this training and energy-building the athlete will not run well, and certainly he or she cannot win!

Perhaps the simplest definition of energy is *the capacity to do work*. As such, it is as important as strategy. For you can have a good strategy, but if you haven't the energy to implement it, you will achieve little. It has been said that, although Apple was able to imagine the future in desk and lap top computing, it was unable to build it. So Bill Gates stepped in and built the future Apple foresaw, making himself the richest man in the world.

The energy envisaged in verse 5 is the energy to win! 'An athlete who runs in a race cannot win the prize unless he obeys the rules.' And winning is as important in life and in business as it is in sport. According to John Kotter, one of today's management 'gurus', 'The notion of wanting to be best at something is a far more common theme in successful business visions than most people realise.'

In today's world, the energy to change is as vital as the energy to persevere and win in the pursuit of our goals. For in a 'corporate environment changing at warp speed' (*The Corporate Athlete*, Harvard Business Review, January, 2001), proactive and reactive flexibility is vital on the part of UBS and Bible Societies. 'In an increasingly competitive global market place, it is hard to imagine slow and cumbersome bureaucratic organisations becoming the best at anything.' (John Kotter). This surely is a challenge to all networked organisations, like UBS, which believe in maximising consultation. One of the challenges we will increasingly face will be:

Can UBS and Bible Society *minutes* keep pace with God's kairos *moments*?

Our task in building the future imagined at Midrand will be hard work! It will demand a lot of energy. It will require a high level of commitment from all of us.

The Corporate Athlete article speaks of the need for energy management, if high levels of energy are to be maintained. According to this article, there are two key components in energy management.

The first is to ensure that there is a rhythmic movement in our behaviour between energy expenditure [stress] and energy renewal [recovery]. It calls this movement 'oscillation'.

The second is to practice rituals that promote oscillation. The article gives examples of such 'rituals' at four levels – the physical, emotional, mental and spiritual.

It will be vital for us to recognise the importance of energy and energy management, if we are to move forward as a Fellowship. We will be able to expend great amounts of energy if we take time to renew it. Only if we do that, will be able to say with John Whitefield, the 18th century Anglican evangelist: 'I never feel better than when I'm on the full stretch for God.'

Farmer

The third image reinforces the need for energy to be expended. The farmer is described as the one 'who has done the hard work' (v.6). The nuance I wish to underline in this farming metaphor is brought out in the Parable of the Growing Seed in Mark 4.26-29:

> A man scatters seed in his field. He sleeps at night, is up and about during the day, and all the while the seeds are sprouting and growing. Yet he does not know how it happens. The soil itself makes the plants grow and bear fruit.

Jesus stresses the *efficacy* of the agricultural process. 'The seeds are sprouting and growing.' But this happens not because of the farmer, but because of the soil. In fact, the farmer 'does not know how it happens.'

The farmer works hard, but nature also is at work, causing the seed to sprout and grow. And without the work of nature, the hard work of the farmer in tilling the soil and sowing the seed would be in vain. The focus is on *efficacy* – on that which makes the farmer's work fruitful.

This parable, like all Jesus' parables, is a parable of the Kingdom, or Kingship of God, i.e. it illustrates the activity of God in the world. It tells us that it is *God* who makes the seed of the Word to sprout, grow and bear fruit in human lives!

Surely this biblical principle is very relevant to Bible work. We can translate, publish and distribute the Scriptures; we can produce the finest helps for readers, hearers and viewers so that they interact with the text. But unless the Holy

Spirit animates the sacred text, the voice of God will not be heard. We can work hard and long, and impress others, but unless the Holy Spirit blesses our labours, our work will have no lasting impact. We are co-workers with God. But if the chief worker is absent, nothing will be achieved!

This is why faith, prayer, worship and doxology are such vital features of our corporate life in Bible Societies and the UBS as well as of our church life, family life and personal life. For they are a formal recognition that without Christ we can do nothing (cf John 15.5).

As we in our Bible Societies and in the UBS re-evaluate and update our strategies to fulfil the four-year strategic direction set by the Midrand Assembly, may all Board members and all staff resolve to set this process in:

- A Biblical context
- A Church context
- A Business context

The challenge all of us face is:

- To build the future of yesterday (World Assembly 2000)
- To imagine the future of tomorrow (World Assembly 2004)

In developing a strategy to achieve this, may God grant us the energy we need and the efficacy we cannot do without!

July 2001   PRIDE

`Paediatrician, biographer, poet and musician'

This headline in *The Herald*, one of the Scottish broadsheets, last May caught my attention. The accompanying photograph immediately activated long term memory banks, and events of 40 years ago flooded back into mind.

The heading stood above an obituary article announcing the death at the age of 93 of a remarkable lady. I first knew her many years ago when, as a university student, I visited Vancouver, Canada, to undertake a summer preaching placement. Both going and returning, I travelled across Canada from coast to coast by train, spending a day or two at various places en route. The second last leg of my return journey was from Thunder Bay, on the northern shore of Lake Ontario, to Toronto. On boarding the train, I was surprised to find Dr Jean MacLennan, a medical doctor and active member of the church in Vancouver where a week previously I had completed my placement.

This lady, who had emigrated in mid-life to Canada from the UK some ten years earlier, was a great conversationalist, and as the train trundled past forest and lake I was regaled with stories of her youth in London and of her family's annual summer pilgrimage to the Scottish Highlands. The anonymous writer in *The Herald* summed her up well: 'With a wonderful memory and a rich store of anecdotes, she was delightful company.'

What most stands out in my memories of that train journey is Dr MacLennan's sharing her recollections of an article on Pride which she told me she had read as a teenager. The author of the article apparently identified four types of pride: Pride of face, pride of place, pride of race and pride of grace.

Pride – one of the seven deadly sins! Pride – the acid that corrodes spirituality! Pride – the poison which enfeebles the Body of Christ!

This month let's take a quick look at these four 'pride types' and also take heart from a biblical antidote for each!

Pride of Face

For centuries pride of face has been a snare, both to the one whose face it is, and to those who find the face attractive. But our current western obsession with bodily health and physical appearance seems to be making it particularly potent today. This was illustrated in reverse during the recent British General Election. *The Herald* – on another day and by a different writer – complained that one of the political leaders, whom it described as 'a decent, committed man' was 'dismantled (by the media) in embarrassingly slow motion because he is bald and speaks in a funny voice.'

Today being photogenic covers a multitude of sins! That's why it may be time to rediscover the words of the Lord to Samuel: People judge others by what they look like, but I judge people by what is in their hearts (1 Samuel 16.7, CEV). It is how the Lord sees us that counts!

Antidote: The shining Face. *[May] the Lord turn his face toward you and give you peace!* (Numbers 6.26, NRSV)

Pride of Place

Pride of place is potent because place equates with power. And the will to power remains a dominant human motivation. There is, of course, a legitimate pride in personal achievement, which alas! those with a low sense of self-worth fail to enjoy. But if we achieve in order to look down on others or to manipulate them, our achievement becomes a Tower of Babel rather than a Temple of Zion.

All of us – especially those who are achievers – need to meditate deeply on St Paul's words to the Philippians:

Think the same way as Christ Jesus thought:

Christ was truly God.

But did not try to remain equal with God.

He gave up everything and became a slave,

when he became like one of us.   (Philippians 2.5-7, CEV)

Antidote: The empty throne. *He gave up everything* (Phil 2.7).

Pride of Race

The ongoing process of globalisation is today producing mass migrations of peoples in search of work, scattering millions far from their homelands. As a result there are large multiracial areas in many cities where tensions all too easily boil over. In such situations Christians are called to witness to the One who 'from one human being he created all races on earth' (Acts 17.26, GNB), and churches are challenged to demonstrate that 'the body of Christ has many different parts, as any other body does', and to proclaim to the wider community:

God's Spirit is inside each of us, and all around us as well. So it doesn't matter that some of us are Jews and others are Gentiles and that some are slaves and others are free. Together we are one body.

{1 Corinthians 12.13, CEVmg)

Antidote: The broken wall. *Christ has united us by breaking down the wall of hatred that separated us.* (Ephesians 2.14, CEV)

Pride of Grace

This fourth pride, I remember Dr Jean reminding me as the train rattled on, is the worst of all. To be proud of having received God's undeserved mercy is illogical. But worse, it is lethal to any latent Christ-like spirituality God may have sown in our hearts! And yet, does not this very pride lie at the root of so much of the confessional and denominational exclusiveness which prevents many Christians from embracing one another as brothers and sisters in the Lord?

This was the besetting sin of the religious establishment Jesus had to deal with. Do you remember the story he told 'to some people who thought they were better than others and who looked down on everyone else'? It is about a Pharisee and a tax collector. Both went to the temple to pray. Jesus tells us:

The Pharisee stood over by himself and prayed…. `I am really glad that I am not like that tax collector over there.'

In marked contrast:

> The tax collector.... was so sorry for what he had done that he pounded his chest and prayed, `God have pity on me! I am such a sinner.'

Jesus' verdict? 'It was the tax collector and not the Pharisee who was pleasing to God.'

The lesson? 'If you put yourself above others, you will be put down. But if you humble yourself, you will be honoured.' (Luke 18.9-14, CEV)

Antidote: The basic prayer. *God have pity on me! I am such a sinner.* (Luke 18.13)

To wind up this month, here are some quotes on pride.

> A proud man is always looking down on things and people; and, of course, as long as you're looking down, you can't see something that's above you.   - C S Lewis

> God sends no one away empty except those who are full of themselves.
>   - Dwight L Moody

> Pride and grace dwell never in one place.
>   - Thomas Fuller

> You can have no greater sign of a confirmed pride than when you think you are humble enough.
>   - William Law

August 2001   KING JAMES VERSION

I don't suppose many of you have ever heard of `Burntisland'.

Burntisland is a small town on the east coast of Scotland which has three claims to fame:

-   In 1850 it became the terminus of the first rail ferry in the world.
-   In the 18th century it offered the best British North Sea harbour between London and Orkney.
-   In 1601 the General Assembly of the Church of Scotland meeting there in the presence of King James and with his enthusiastic support, took an initiative which eventually led to the publication of the King James Bible some 10 years later.

There is no doubt which of these three achievements has been the most influential! In June this year the whole community of Burntisland celebrated the town's link with the King James Version in a series of events which centred on commemorative services in Burntisland Kirk on all four Sundays of the month, but also involved the wider community, especially the local schools. Dolina and I had the privilege of attending the final service of commemoration on 23 June at which the Moderator of the General Assembly preached, with the Catholic Archbishop of St Andrews and Edinburgh, the Episcopal Primus and the Executive Director of the Scottish Bible Society also taking part.

It was a memorable occasion enhanced by falling on a magnificent summer's day and taking place within an ancient, but newly and very beautifully, restored parish church. But the sudden death of Cardinal Tom Winning of Glasgow cast a shadow over the event, for he was due to take part in the service and, indeed, had been the published preacher for the previous Sunday. A sudden heart attack meant that he had been unable to preach, but his sermon had been prepared and he arranged for Monsignor Peter Smith to deliver it in his place.

Sadly when Monsignor Smith was driving to Burntisland to carry out this task he got a mobile phone call to say that the Cardinal had died. He felt he had to return to Glasgow immediately, but first visited a local police station and requested the police to fax the text of the sermon to the police station in Burntisland which, in turn, had it delivered it to the church in time for the service! There the sermon was read by Gillian Paterson, an elder in Burntisland Kirk and the organiser of the month-long celebration.

Such dramatic circumstances meant that the Cardinal's sermon on the King James Bible got extensive media coverage. As well it should, for it was a great sermon. Let me share part of it with you!

As a cardinal of the Roman Catholic Church, I do not hesitate to give thanks for the beauty, the power, and the language of the King James Bible. I do not hesitate to give thanks for all those people who have been inspired by this translation of the Sacred Texts and who, thus inspired, have given witness to their faith in Jesus Christ as Lord and Saviour.

Few books – perhaps only the works of Shakespeare come close – have shaped our language so profoundly. In shaping our language, the King James version has also shaped our society and influenced properly our Scottish and English ways of thinking.

Here in Burntisland four centuries ago, a very significant step was taken in building a Christian civilisation which has weathered the storms of the years. But that storm still rages and our society needs to hear God's Word and be challenged by the values of God's kingdom and the person of Jesus Christ.

Tom Winning was an outstanding Christian leader and a warm hearted person, as well as a good friend of the Scottish Bible Society. He will be deeply missed, for he provided forthright leadership on many public issues, not only to the Catholic community, but also to the whole Church in Scotland. And today I suspect he may be indulging in a wry smile that his Burntisland sermon – delivered by a woman Presbyterian elder within minutes of his death – means that the last public utterance of a Catholic cardinal was a glowing commendation of the King James Bible!

The King James Bible continues to enjoy remarkable popularity in the English speaking world. This may well be because it was translated when the English language was at a high point in its development; those who produced the Revised Version in 1881 paid tribute to `the music of its cadences and the felicities of its rhythm'. It deeply influenced English literature and popular speech which even today continue to borrow from it a host of memorable phrases, such as `the skin of my teeth' (Job 19.20), `the salt of the earth' (Matthew 5.13) and `the powers that be' (Romans 13.1). It also extensively influenced other languages, for the King James Bible became an important source text for early translations of the Scriptures into many African and some Asian languages.

The remarkable impact the King James Bible in its heyday made on the public life of the English-speaking nations is in marked contrast with the present marginalisation of the Bible in most western countries today. Let me share three examples of this I came across recently.

- On 24 June *The Daily Telegraph* of London published an article on the KJV in which the writer confessed: `Few of my colleagues have read the Bible. An illiterate housewife in the 15th century knew more than they of it, through the homilies of the parish priest, and through Bible stories from the Golden Legend and other popular collections.'

- A feature entitled `The Silenced Word' appeared last March in the North American journal *Christianity Today* in which the writer lamented the growing trend in evangelical churches to omit Scripture reading altogether as an act of worship. In church life as well as public life the Bible seems to be discounted today!

- The cover story of the June/July issue of the ABS Record features an interview with George Gallup, the American pollster. `We revere the Bible,' he says. `But we don't read it.' This verdict is based on repeated surveys of Americans' knowledge of Scripture.

All of this serves to underline the importance of Bible use. Scripture engagement has always been the objective of translating and publishing the

Bible. Listen to John Wycliffe:

I have translated the New Testament for your spiritual edifying, consolation and solace. Give diligence, reader, I exhort thee… create afresh and enjoy the fruits of the blood of Christ.

And today, Scripture engagement is more vital than ever. Listen once more to George Gallup:

The challenge of the churches in the new millennium, he says, is to forge `free floating spirituality into religious commitment'. Christians can fill the void. `If they can ignite biblical faith,' he says, `there is no telling what impact it might have.'

The best way to celebrate the great Bible translation and publishing events of the past is precisely to help ignite a biblical faith in more and more people so that they discover that `the Bible is a way of liberation.' (Gallup again!)

Finally, we ought not to overlook the fact that to the great majority of the 300 million English speakers in the world today, the cadence and felicities of the KJV are a strange tongue. This is hardly surprising because, not only has the number of English speakers grown enormously (there were little more than 5 million in 1601!), but the language has also changed significantly over the last four centuries.

However, as Mark Twain reminds us, the key challenge lies not in the parts of the Bible we cannot understand, but in those that we do!

September 2001   FUND-RAISING

I want to begin this month by asking two questions:
- Is `fund-raising' a word that excites you, turns you on?
- Is the church offering an inspiring part of the Sunday service for you?

I want to suggest that these two questions are connected. You cannot be a good fund-raiser unless you are a good donor!

The *Direction from Midrand* sets fund-raising in the wider biblical context of Christian stewardship – the stewardship of shared resources of people, money and knowledge. A narrower view, which would see it as a subject in its own right, runs the risk of losing the biblical perspective which is all important when dealing with money.

This wider context is reinforced by the *UBS Identity and Ethos* statement. There fund-raising is described, not as an end in itself, but as a means of enabling Bible Societies to fulfil their mission to make the Bible accessible and affordable to all. Fund-raising thus becomes one of the key components making up the foundation of a Bible Society. And it is on this foundation that Bible Societies build the pillars of Scripture translation, distribution and engagement

I am convinced that when our fund-raising reflects the biblical perspective suggested by Midrand we raise more money! In addition, we find fund-raising to be an honour, not a burden. It becomes a beautiful, spiritual and enjoyable activity!

Money can be raised only as it is given. So it's not surprising that most of the relevant biblical teaching focuses on *giving*. But the Bible also sees *raising* funds as vital. St Paul emerges as an enthusiastic fund-raiser! He knew how to make a persuasive `ask'! But his fund-raising authenticity was less a matter of technique - good as that was - than of example. His audiences knew that he personally donated his own support as a Christian missionary (Acts 20.34; 1Corinthians 9.6). He could testify to the deep sense of fulfilment giving gave to him (Acts 20.35).

So, what is the Bible's teaching on giving? I think three phrases sum this up. Together they make up what we might call the `Facets of Philanthropy.'

It's bountiful

In his fund-raising letter to the Corinthians, St Paul held up the example of the Macedonian Christians to the north. `They were extremely generous in their giving' he tells the Corinthians, `even though they were very poor.' (2 Corinthians 8.2, GNB) The story in the gospels of the widow's offering to the temple treasury underlines that our generosity is relative to the size of our resources. Her two little copper coins were worth more in the eyes of Jesus than all the large gifts of some major donors!

In other words, Christian giving is serious! It's not donating small change we will never miss. We can't be `generous' without feeling the pinch! Generosity implies an element of sacrifice (2 Corinthians 8.12). On the other hand, however generous you may be to Christian causes, you're unlikely to end up bankrupt! For `God is able to give you more than you need, so that you will always have all you need for yourselves and more than enough for every good cause.' (2 Corinthians 9.8, GNB)

None of us is too poor to make a gift! For `He [God] will always make you rich enough to be generous at all times, so that many will thank God for your gifts.' (2 Corinthians 9.11, GNB)

It's beautiful

One of the most remarkable (and generous) acts of giving recorded in the Bible was the donation of the jar of expensive perfume for Jesus' anointing at Bethany. Jesus called it `a fine and beautiful thing' (Matthew 26.10, GNB). And in 1 Corinthians 16.3, St Paul, describing the gift of the Corinthians for the poor Christians in Jerusalem, uses the Greek word *charis*, a word often translated `grace', but containing the basic meaning of beauty or attractiveness. Again, the apostle regarded the gift sent by the Philippians as `a fragrant offering' (Philippians 4.8).

Sacrificial giving is beautiful when it expresses true love and genuine compassion. For then it reflects the loveliness of the grace of our Lord Jesus Christ. `Rich as he was, he made himself poor for your sake, in order to make you rich by means of his poverty.' (2 Corinthians 8.9, GNB) Giving is part of our worship of God Almighty! A tangible response to his great love and mercy!

Charitable giving is sometimes regarded as tacky, lacking in respectability. But Jesus and St Paul see it differently. For them it is something noble and attractive because it reflects the caring heart of God across social and ethnic divisions, bringing genuine delight to givers and recipients.

It's blissful

Far from being a pain, Christian giving is a joy! It's a blessing to the giver as much as to the receiver! When urging some local church leaders to help the weak, St Paul reminded them of an otherwise unrecorded saying of Jesus: `More blessings come from giving than from receiving.' (Acts 20.35, CEV) The apostle reported to the Greeks that the Macedonians `were glad to give generously' and that `they even asked and begged us to let them have the joy of giving their money for God's people.' (2 Corinthians 8.2,4 CEV) Paul also emphasised to the Corinthians that giving flows from the gospel rather than from the law: `You should give, then, as you have decided, not with regret or out of a sense of duty; for God loves the one who gives gladly.' (2 Corinthians 9.7, GNB) This last word `gladly' translates the Greek *hilaros*, from which we get the term `hilarity' – hardly an idea which modern westerners tend to associate with Christian giving! African Christians seem to be more in tune with St Paul, for in many of their churches the offering is a real highlight in the worship service.

But in fact people everywhere can – and do – enjoy philanthropy! That's why the most persuasive fund-raisers are happy donors! If we – be we Bible

Society staff, Board members or volunteers – are ourselves already generous donors to the Bible Society, this invariably imparts an invisible, but powerful, authenticity to our act of asking others to give to the Bible cause. Why did King Hezekiah's appeal for his program of spiritual renewal in Jerusalem receive a bumper response? Because he first gave of his own resources before asking the people to donate theirs (2 Chronicles 31.2-10)!

The three 'Facets of Philanthropy' provide a key checklist when we make an offering to the Church, the Bible Society or to any other good cause. I wonder, how do we measure up?

The 'Facets' also suggest some key features of Christian fund-raising, such as:
- touching hearts, rather than twisting arms
- building trust, not producing guilt
- providing opportunity for service, instead of taking advantage of generosity
- helping donors find fulfilment and feel that they belong

Fund-raising ought not to be seen as an optional extra for Bible Societies. It is must not be treated as the poor relation of other Bible Society activities! In a sense, all of us involved in the Bible cause are fund-raisers because our commitment and enthusiasm [or lack of these] influence people we meet to give, or not to give, to the cause we represent. May all of us be enthusiastic, not reluctant fund-raisers!

At the Midrand Assembly the Fellowship committed itself to: 'Increase the money available for the world wide work through strengthening the fund-raising capacity of each Bible Society' (*The Direction from Midrand*). Let us all do our utmost to turn this commitment into a reality!

October 2001   IMAGINATION

I want to begin this month with three quotations.

'For 2 and 2 make 4 is not a part of life, but the beginning of death'
- Fyodor Dostoevsky, 19th century Russian novelist

'The soul without imagination is what an observatory would be without a telescope'
- Henry Ward Beecher, 19th century American Congregational preacher

'The church on Sunday morning… may be the last place left in our society for imaginative speech that permits people to enter into new worlds of faith and to participate in joyous, obedient life.'
- Walter Brueggemann, contemporary American biblical scholar

Now allow me to follow up these three quotations with two questions:
- How vivid is your imagination?
- Does your imagination help you interact with the Scriptures?

These are important questions for three reasons.

First, because the biblical text is clearly designed to engage our human imagination by employing gripping narrative, vivid metaphor, evocative parables, symbolic signs, intense poetry, etc.

Second, because in our world of visual media, the imagination of many has become atrophied. In his book *Under the Unpredictable Plant*, Eugene Peterson warns that when imagination is neurotic and sluggish, `it turns people, millions of them, into parasites, copycats, and couch potatoes' (p.171).

Third, for Christians imagination is indispensable. Peterson underlines this eloquently. `We who are made in the *"image"* of God have, as a consequence, *imag*-ination. Imagination is the capacity to make connections between the visible and the invisible, between heaven and earth, between present and past, between present and future' (p.169f).

Karl Marx and King James

Yet sadly imagination is marginalised in western churches. The two principle culprits are Karl Marx and the King James Version! These unlikely bed fellows have reinforced one another with powerful effect!

Marx contended that religion is an engineered illusion thought up to distract and divert the masses from the misery of their situation. Therefore, Christians have tended to react by down playing the role of imagination in faith.

Two centuries before Marx, the KJV translators betrayed a bias against imagination in their use of the term. All of the 19 occurrences of *imagination* in the KJV are adverse. I need quote only two to illustrate this negativity.

- In Genesis 6.5, the reason for the Flood is *that every imagination of the thoughts of his heart was only evil continually*.

- And Romans 1.21 tells us that one of the reasons why the wrath of God is revealed is because people *became vain in their imaginations, and their foolish heart was darkened*.

Significantly modern English translations use alternatives like `inclinations' and `thinking'.

Today in our unimaginative media culture we urgently need to rehabilitate and rediscover how to use our imagination, not least when engaging with the Scriptures. `Right now, one of the essential Christian ministries in and to our ruined world is the recovery and exercise of the imagination' (Eugene Peterson, p.171).

115

Not only does the Bible employ imagination in the communication of the Word of God to us. It encourages us to use it in order to hear God speak to us! No modern biblical scholar makes this point more strongly than Walter Brueggemann. In his commentary on *Jeremiah*, he strongly argues that we cannot hear the message of the prophet unless we allow the power of his imagery to assault our imagination.

Imaginative characterization

Brueggemann illustrates his point from Jeremiah 5.15-17: *People of Israel, the LORD is bringing a nation from afar to attack you.* Brueggeman contends that the attempts by many commentators to identify this nation miss the point: `It is futile for us to try to identify the specific army from the general description, because the language is not descriptive but imaginative characterization. Its purpose is not to communicate information but to create a sense in the listening community of what it is like to be on the receiving end of such an army. The poetic scenario invites Jerusalem to receive God's judgment ahead of the fact of military invasion' (*To Pluck Up, To Tear Down: Jeremiah 1-25*).

One of the ways of imaginatively engaging with the Scriptures is through meditative reading.

There are numerous occasions when the Bible urges us to meditate on the text. One of these is Psalm 119.48: `I respect and love your commandments, I will meditate on your instructions' (GNB). In English versions the noun *meditation* or the verb *to meditate* is found 10 times in the GNB (all in the Psalms) and 19 times in the KJV (15 of these in the Psalms).

Yet meditation is not highly ranked in much western spirituality. Perhaps two of the main reasons why meditation is not popular is because...

·   We tend to associate the word *meditation* with `Transcendental Meditation' - the technique of detaching oneself from anxiety and promoting self-realisation and harmony by meditation, repetition of mantras and other practices.

·   Our tendency when reading the Bible is to focus on the *meaning* of the text rather than its *message*. We study, analyse the text in order to discover its meaning, rather than allowing the text impact us.

Stepping into the text

Meditation is more than study of the text. Richard Foster helps us to see this when he says that in study we step back from the text, while in meditation we step into it. Our imagination first helps us to enter the biblical story and then to discover ways in which God's Word can enable us to live today. An imaginative approach also makes it less likely that we try `to control' the outcome of our encounter with text by allowing it speak to us only at the cerebral level. And it also makes us more open to encounter God himself and hear him speak to us through his Word.

Thank God there are signs of an awakening new interest in imaginative approaches to the biblical text! Some devotees suggest that the naïve, imaginative approach ought to take precedence over the more analytical. They argue that, if we do not obey until we understand, we are in danger of allowing the text to die the death of a thousand qualifications! But the evidence from Psalm 119 suggests that the meditative and the cognitive may alternately take the lead. In verse 99, meditation leads to understanding.

I understand more than all my teachers,
because I meditate on your instructions.

But in verse 27 the cognitive precedes the meditative:

Help me to understand your laws,
and I will meditate on your wonderful teachings.

So probably it's wiser to opt for a `both/and' rather than an `either/or' approach. We need to be open to both, sometimes following one and sometimes the other, and always holding both together in creative tension. Peterson helpfully says that imagination and explanation are designed to work in tandem: `Explanation keeps our feet on the ground; Imagination lifts our head in the clouds.' (p.171)

Aids to meditation

According to Thomas Merton in his book *Contemplative Prayer*, most of us have to learn to meditate. How, then, do we learn?

Here are three basic suggestions:

- First `Be still'. Stilling our busy lives helps us sense the presence of God (Psalm 46.10). This is why many Church Fathers in the early centuries lived as hermits in the deserts of Egypt and North Africa. It is also why silent spiritual `retreats' are beneficial in creating space in our hectic modern lives to listen to God.

- Second, `Be patient'. 'I waited patiently for the Lord's help; then he listened to me and heard my cry' (Psalm 40.1). God's blessing is seldom available on demand! `We must wait for God, long, meekly, in the wind and wet, in the thunder and lightning, in the cold and the dark. Wait, and he will come. He never comes to those who do not wait' (Frederick Faber).

- Third, `Be prayerful'. As we meditate on Scripture we will find ourselves moving naturally into prayer. Martin Smith SSJE in his book *The Word is very near you: A guide to praying with Scripture*, speaks of `meditative prayer' flowing from meditative reading, and I want to conclude by sharing with you some of his understanding of this type of prayer.

Meditative prayer

Smith contends that meditative prayer is a two-way conversation.

> In meditative prayer we deliberately open ourselves to hearing God's word to us, sensing God's touch, accepting God's gift and allow ourselves to respond simply to that experience. This particular type of meditative prayer is one that uses the Scriptures as the medium for God's self-disclosure and gift (p.25).

> In meditative prayer I give God an opportunity to begin a new conversation with myself by entering one of the conversations now embedded in our Scriptures (p.55).

He goes on to emphasise that meditative prayer involves imagination as well as reason.

> It is `a kind of praying that does not confine itself to the surface levels of reasoning and talking and thinking. It won't be a matter of the head, and tidy, controlled conversations with the Lord. This kind of praying will involve the inner world where the invisible springs of our actions lie, it will penetrate to levels of deep need, disturbance, feeling, levels where we are hurt and warped, and levels where we have wants not at all satisfied by conventional palliatives, and gifts waiting to come out of bud' (p.43).

Smith underlines the prompting role of the Holy Spirit in meditative prayer.

> Meditative prayer with Scripture is the art of absorbing, taking in image after image of Scripture so that the Spirit within us can impress the deepest levels of our being with their meaning. In meditative prayer the Spirit makes the connection between our deepest needs and the images that answer them and convey the grace and touch of God's power. In meditating on the images of Scripture our inarticulate feelings find expression for themselves so that they can come to the surface and be consciously offered to God (p.45).

Meditation has for centuries been regarded as one of the `disciplines' of classical Christian spirituality. Surely the time has come to rediscover this tradition and root it in our 21st century encounter with the Word of God!

November 2001   9 - 11

I write one week after the appalling terrorist attacks on the World Trade Center towers in Manhattan and the Pentagon in Washington. The impact on the world has been phenomenal. And there may be more to come, either by way of reprisal or tit-for-tat escalation. These are very unsettling times and they underline that our ministry in the Bible cause is more urgent than ever.

The American Bible Society produced with remarkable speed a special Scripture portion in English and Spanish entitled *God is our Shelter and Strength*. It is a superb production containing extensive Scripture texts grouped around the felt needs of the American people at this time.

In addition to the Scripture text, there are helpful questions at the conclusion to each chapter to help users engage with 'Words of Assurance'.

Many hundreds of thousands of copies are being used across the United States and I know that our global family is praying that these words of comfort and strength may bring hope to thousands of people passing through a period of great trial.

Ultimately the only answer to all acts of terrorism and the perceived injustices and frustrations provoking them, is a re-discovery by ordinary people - across cultures and religions - of the truths contained in God's Word. On reflecting on the current crisis, it struck me that Jews, Christians and Muslims all place great value on the Psalms of David. So perhaps it is in these ancient inspired poems that an effective ministry of reconciliation might begin. With that thought in mind, I offer this month a meditation on themes from the Book of Psalms, grouped under six headlines highlighted by recent events.[1]

Life is fragile

For the psalmist, life at its best is frail.

> As for us, our life is like grass. We grow and flourish like a wild flower; then the wind blows on it, and it is gone – no one sees it again. (Psalm 103.15,16)

The Bible captures the fragility of human existence in a series of graphic images – 'a passing shadow' (1Chronicles 29.15); 'a weaver's shuttle' (Job 7.6); 'a puff of wind...a shadow' (Psalm 39.5,6); 'a tent about to be taken down' (Isaiah 38.12) and 'a puff of smoke' (James 4.14).

---

[1] All Scripture quotations are from the Good News Bible, unless otherwise indicated

On the other hand, the Psalms stress that God has an eternal purpose for human beings.

You will show me the path that leads to life;
your presence fills me with joy and brings me pleasure for ever. (Psalm 16.11)

Jesus emphasised that human personality is infinitely valuable.

Do people gain anything if they win the whole world but lose their life? Of course not! There is nothing they can give to regain their life. (Mark 8.36-37)

This is why the key to recovery from terrorist attacks wherever they may occur – be it in Manhattan or Jerusalem, Palestine or the Pentagon – is to promote the discovery and/or recovery in personal and public life of biblical values, such as the sanctity of human life, the pre-eminence of justice and the nobility of mercy. These values are also fundamental if the social inequities, which spawn terrorism, are to be seriously addressed and overcome.

Hate is toxic

Sometimes the psalmist gives vent to personal hatred.

O God, how I wish you would kill the wicked!
How I wish violent people would leave me alone!
They say wicked things about you; they speak evil things against your name.
O LORD, how I hate those who hate you! How I despise those who rebel against you!
I hate them with a total hatred; I regard them as my enemies. (139.19-22)

I suspect not a few of us expressed somewhat similar sentiments on 11 September! I do think most of us have a problem with the more outrageous utterances in the Psalter. But these may help us in moments when we find ourselves consumed with hate by encouraging us to take our hatred to God and leave it with him. If you feel hateful, it's more honest to tell God than to try to repress such `unspiritual' emotions. After sharing our hateful feelings with God, we are often better able to manage them.

In addition, if, following the psalmist's example, we immediately go on to ask God to test our thoughts and tell us if there is any evil in us and guide us in the everlasting way, we may well find the hatred dissolving into repentance and a prayer for forgiveness!

There is no doubt that both the Old and the New Testaments regard hatred as a sociological cancer.

- Hate stirs up trouble, but love overlooks all offences.

- Those who say they are in the light, yet hate their brothers and sisters,
are in the darkness to this very hour.'   (Proverbs 10.12; 1 John 2.9)

But this cancer can be healed by love!

Anger is sometimes OK

The immediate reaction of most people on 11 September was anger and outrage.
The minds of many Christians and Jews – yes, and Muslims, too – must have
turned to the Psalms of Complaint which form a significant proportion of the
Old Testament Psalter. These psalms have been called 'songs of disorientation',
for they vehemently express the vulnerability of individuals and communities
who were hurting due to relentless exposure to attacks from enemies, bouts of
illness, and public humiliations.

I am worn out, O LORD; have pity on me!
Give me strength; I am completely exhausted
and my whole being is deeply troubled.
How long, O LORD, will you wait to help me?   (Psalm 6.2-3)

Why are you so far away, O LORD?
Why do you hide yourself when we are in trouble? (Psalm 10.1)

My God, my God, why have you abandoned me?
I have cried desperately for help, but still it does not come. (Psalm 22.1)

William Barclay tells us that there are two Greek words for anger. The first
refers to the burst of anger, which does not last. The second is more sinister
– it describes the smouldering resentment that will not go away. This second
type of anger is never OK! But alas it lies behind so much of the ethnic and
religious violence of today.

Violence is self-defeating

Violence is a boomerang which so often in the end destroys its own perpetrators.

See how wicked people think up evil; they plan trouble and practise
deception.
But in the traps they set for others, they themselves get caught.
So they are punished by their own evil and are hurt by their own
violence.   (Psalm 7.14-16)

The problem is that any commitment to violence is progressive. Reluctant and
occasional use of violence – even in a good cause - so often degenerates into
dependence on and even enthusiasm for violence. One of the most sobering
utterances of the psalmist is that the Lord hates with all his heart 'those who
love violence'. (Psalm 11.5, NIV)

It is precisely because violence is contagious that, in opposing it, we have to be careful lest we ourselves become violent. The use of force to contain violence can so easily become excessive and degenerate into violence. Solomon's advice remains relevant 3,000 years on: `Don't be jealous of violent people, or decide to act as they do.' (Proverbs 3.31)

Once we resort to violence, we're on the slippery slope! For all of us have sinful hearts which, says Jesus, produce `the evil ideas which lead people to kill' (Matthew 15.19). Surely we all need to heed the Lord's warning to Peter: `All who take the sword will die by the sword.' (Matthew 26.52 cf John 18.10)

Prayer is powerful

Many of the lament psalms are also songs of faith. Again and again, the psalmists move from a starting point of overwhelming anguish and misery into a quiet, and sometimes exuberant, confidence in God's protection.

We see this transition from misery to doxology in Psalm 6. It begins:

O LORD, do not rebuke me in your anger,
or discipline me in your wrath.
Be gracious to me, O LORD, for I am languishing;
O LORD, heal me, for my bones are shaking with terror.
My soul is also struck with terror, while you, O LORD – how long?
(Psalm 6.1-3, NRSV)

Then daringly the speaker bluntly requests the Lord to act:

Turn... save... deliver!

This request is made, not `for my sake', or because I deserve it, or because you owe it to me, but, rather, `for the sake of your steadfast love.' (v.4). The psalmist urges God to uphold his reputation! He presents his need as the Lord's opportunity!

By the end of the poem the terror has gone:

The LORD has heard my supplication: the LORD accepts my prayer.
All my enemies shall be ashamed and struck with terror;
they shall turn back, and in a moment be put to shame.
(Psalm 6.9,10, NRSV)

Between such starts and finishes in the lament psalms there's often a lot of emotional and sometimes, outrageous dialogue. But apparently the Lord doesn't mind blunt prayer talk!

Such movements of the human spirit from fear to faith are examples of what Mother Teresa described as `Prayer enlarging the heart until it is capable of containing God's gift of himself.'

Love is persuasive

In the songs of lament the poet's only hope is the unfailing love of the LORD. We've already noted this in Psalm 6. Here are some samples of the many others:

Don't let my enemies say, 'We have defeated him.'
Don't let them gloat over my downfall.
I rely on your constant love;
I will be glad because you will rescue me.   (Psalm 13.4,5)

Reveal your wonderful love and save me;
at your side I am safe from my enemies.   (Psalm 17.7)

I will be glad and rejoice because of your constant love.
You see my suffering; you know my trouble.   (Psalm 31.7)

Love is the fundamental motive of Christian behaviour. There is not a situation where it can safely be discarded! There are four categories of people that Christians are commanded to love:

- One another. 'And now I give you a new commandment: love one another. As I have loved you, so you must love one another.' (John 13.34; cf 15.12)

- Neighbours. 'Love your neighbour as you love yourself.' (Leviticus 19.18) Jesus called this the second great commandment. (Matthew 22.29)

- Refugees. 'Show love for foreigners, because you were once foreigners in Egypt.' (Deuteronomy 10.19)

- Enemies. 'You have heard that it was said, "Love your friends, hate your enemies." But now I tell you: love your enemies and pray for those who persecute you, so that you may become the children of your Father in heaven.' (Matthew 5.43-45)

Christian love is primarily an act of will rather than an emotion. The power to love against the emotional grain is a gift of God, who himself loved us while we were enemies. (Romans 5.8-10)

Such love is the ultimate argument for Christianity. `If you have love for one another,' says Jesus, `then everyone will know that you are my disciples.' (John 13.35). Our Lord's prayer for his disciples is that we may be one, so that the world will believe that God sent him. (John 17.21)

Let's pray that this love may be demonstrated convincingly in our fearful world!

The Psalms are not limited to a particular age, country, or form of faith. As we engage with them together, the spirit of controversy retreats and confessional conflict drifts into the background. Perhaps that is why ABS portion *God is our Shelter and Strength*, has selected over half of its texts from this ancient hymnbook of humanity.

123

December 2001 WHY BE A VOLUNTEER?

We are now well into Advent and increasingly our thoughts focus on the birth of our Lord and Saviour Jesus Christ. What a tragedy that in the run-up to Christmas this year, Bethlehem has suffered violence and bloodshed on a scale comparable to the massacre of the innocents by King Herod! What a travesty that the celebration of the birth in Bethlehem of the One whose destiny is to bring peace on earth is likely to be disrupted by bombs and bullets!

The conflict which tragically is tearing the Holy Land apart is about *possessing* – possessing the West Bank. The unique birth which occurred in Bethlehem just over two millennia ago had all to do with *giving*. St Paul employs eloquent poetry to remind us that in his advent, Christ gave up everything.

Christ was truly God.
but he did not try to remain equal with God.
He gave up everything, and became a slave,
when he became like one of us.

Christ was humble.
He obeyed God and even died on a cross.
Then God gave Christ the highest place
and honoured his name above all others.

So at the name of Jesus everyone will bow down,
those in heaven, on earth, and under the earth.
And to the glory of God the Father
everyone will openly agree,
Jesus Christ is Lord!' (Philippians 2.6-11, CEV)

The prevailing commercialisation and consumerisation of Christmas can subtly benumb our souls to the stupendous and glorious nature of the incarnation! Only creative interaction with biblical texts and active participation in communal worship will enable us to discover anew the true meaning of Christmas! All over the world it is the enormous privilege of Bible Societies to participate in this Christian counter-culture by providing special Christmas Scripture selections for use by the churches and individuals. Let us support one another by praying that the Holy Spirit might use every selection distributed this Christmas to speak powerfully to all readers and hearers!

The message of Christmas is vital to the Bible Societies. This is true in more than a general sense. The action of Christ in being born into the human race was not only *effective* in leading to our salvation. It was also *exemplary* as the ultimate model of self-giving. Christ was the volunteer *par excellence*! He also successfully persuaded others to give themselves to benevolent service – his disciples were the first Christian volunteers!

We are essentially a volunteer movement

The vital importance of this to the Bible Societies becomes clear when we remember that we are essentially a volunteer movement, quite different from government agencies and commercial enterprises. True, we employ paid staff to coordinate our programs. But it is volunteers who offer the prayers, donate the money, provide the governance, advocate the cause and achieve much of the distribution.

Bible Societies serve the churches and are essentially church-related organisations. And yet they are not owned by any single church, denomination or confession. They are akin to the missionary band of St Paul in the early church who travelled with him from place to place communicating the Good News. Ralph Winter the Californian missiologist considers the Pauline missionary band as a prototype of all subsequent missionary endeavours organised by committed church members over and above their commitment to their local church.

From the beginning, involvement in the Bible Society called for a `second decision' over and above the decision to adhere to the church. The earliest Bible Society was structured as a grass roots volunteer movement through the creation of a network of local Bible Societies or `auxiliaries.' The members of these local bodies were mainly fundraising volunteers who challenged and encouraged others to support the work of Bible translation and distribution. In this strong involvement of lay people, the Bible Society was not unique. Stephen Neill, Christian missions historian, informs us that `in all periods from the beginning, "missions" have tended to be an adventure of inspired individuals, of religious orders, of private societies, of groups of "friends of missions."' (*A History of Christian Missions*).

And still today, Christians become Bible Society volunteers by making a conscious decision to give their time, their skills and their resources to advance Bible work at home and abroad.

What is a Bible Society volunteer?

The UBS Volunteers Manual provides the answer:

> Anyone who loves the Bible and has decided to share it, without financial reward, by such activities as Scripture distribution, promotion of the Bible Societies, encouragement of support for the Bible cause, etc.

So the profile of a Bible Society volunteer is a Christian who values the Bible. In addition, a volunteer is a self-starter, is dependable, has the ability to influence others and is endowed with common sense, Where (s)he is a team person who delegates creatively, communicates well and makes things happen, there is potential to become a volunteer group leader.

Obviously, a volunteer must be someone with time as well as talents. But we ought not to hesitate to invite busy people to become volunteers, for they are often the ones who have the greatest capacity to make time available!

Bible Society volunteers symbolise the ethos of the Bible Society movement. 'The Bible Societies are an expression of the fellowship of God's people sharing their resources. These include, for example, spiritual gifts, knowledge, money, time, talents, and technology.' (*UBS Identity and Ethos*, 2000)

Why are volunteers important?

There are eight reasons why volunteers are important.

- People are a Bible Society's most important asset. So, use them! No Bible Society can afford to be a faceless organisation in the local community.

- Face-to-face communication at the grass roots is vitally important, even in an age of mass media. Mail shots need to be supplemented by a more direct and personal approach.

- Volunteer activity nourishes and confirms a sense of belonging to the Bible Society family. Nurturing this sense of belonging is becoming more important in many western societies where long-term volunteering is diminishing.

- People motivate people. Volunteers enable other people catch the vision for the work. According to one Bible Society, 'Volunteers provide spontaneous combustion' to its entire enterprise.

- Distant contact (e.g. by mail, e-mail, telephone) is more susceptible to donor fatigue.

- A volunteer program can be more cost-effective than other means of raising funds. But volunteers require to be managed and performance analysis is essential!

- By identifying appropriate volunteers, Bible Societies benefit from a wide range of skills (e.g. in business, etc.).

- Volunteers enhance the potential of a Bible Society to achieve new levels of performance in fulfilling its mission.

Why become a Bible Society volunteer?

There are many reasons why each of the tens of thousands of Bible Society volunteers around the world have decided to commit their time and their talents to the Bible cause. It would be impossible to list them all here! But I think there are four basic reasons which cover all the others.

Bible Society volunteers...

- *Help to build Christ's Church throughout the world!* A M Chirgwin summed up the history of the Church in one terse phrase: `First a Bible, then a convert, and then a church'.

- *Accelerate the coming of God's Kingdom!* In the Parable of the Sower, Jesus tells us that the Word is the seed of the Kingdom. As it is distributed, received and believed, so God's will is discovered and put into practice.

- *Make the world a better place.* By making God's Word available and accessible we release its values into human society. These are values which emancipate women, outlaw child labour, establish the rights of the poor and respect the integrity of the environment.

- *Find a new freedom.* It is in serving others (not in indulging ourselves!) that we find perfect freedom. Better to find fulfilment as a Bible Society volunteer than suffer frustration as a couch potato! The service that counts is the service that costs!

There's no better way to exemplify the spirit of Advent than to become a Bible Society volunteer!

The Christmas season reminds us of Christ's first step in giving up everything for our salvation. That first step into a manger led to another step on to a cross. It is important to remember that, in taking both momentous steps, Christ acted as a volunteer.

> The Father loves me because I am willing to give up my life, in order that I may receive it back again. No one takes my life away from me. I give it up of my own free will. I have the right to give it up, and I have the right to take it back. This is what my Father has commanded me to do. *(John 10.17-18)*

> In all things he fulfilled his Father's commands. Let us follow in his steps! (1Peter 2.21)

In the run up to Advent I was privileged to preach in All Saints Anglican Cathedral, Nairobi. While waiting for the service to begin, I was struck by a signed photograph hanging outside the Provost's office. It was a picture of

Jim Irwin standing on the moon during the first Apollo lunar landing. The astronaut had personally donated the photograph to the cathedral in 1991, and above his signature had written the following words:

'Jesus walking on earth is more important than man walking on the moon.'

That's why we celebrate Advent!

January 2002   BUILDING THE UBS HOUSE

This is the month to wish you all a `Happy New Year' and I do so very sincerely. Perhaps some of you would prefer me to wish you a `Blessed New Year'! A year or two ago, a Presbyterian elder in Wellington, New Zealand, took me to task after divine service because the Good News Translation uses `Happy' rather than `Blessed' in the Beatitudes! I will always remember the rationale of his preference for the more traditional rendering: `If I want to be happy,' he said, `I can go to the tavern. But if I want to be blessed, I come to church!'

Of course, both words have the same meaning, though `Blessed' has greater religious overtones. But even more important than how we describe this consciousness of God's love, is how we respond to it. God calls us to be more than *consumers* of his blessings! He wants us to be *constructors* as well as consumers! That is, he blesses us in order that out of his blessings we might construct lifestyles of thanksgiving which will bring glory to his name and good to the world.

Certainly, the passing of another milestone in life is an occasion for both doxology and dedication. And I wish to suggest that there is no better way to construct anew our dedication to the Lord and to his service than to resolve by his grace to incarnate in our lives the UBS identity and ethos! When I was General Secretary in Scotland, I used to encourage Bible Society members and supporters to identify with the cause they supported, and say to themselves, `I am the Scottish Bible Society.' And now in this my last New Year greeting as UBS General Secretary, I want to encourage all who read this letter to begin the year 2002, saying to themselves: `I am the UBS!'

The UBS house

Sometimes I think of the UBS – and, indeed, any individual Bible Society - as a house. The UBS house seen by my mind's eye is in the Greek classical style, for it has three pillars. The pillars are: *Scripture translation, distribution* and *engagement.*

Next I notice that these pillars are resting on a triple-layered foundation composed of: *prayer, volunteerism* and *fundraising.*

This mental picture of a building with pillars and foundation sum up for me the great priorities of Bible Societies.

The questions I want to ask us all are:

- Are we concerned to construct this building in terms of who we are as well as of what we do?
- How far does our personal lifestyle exemplify these Bible Society priorities?

I ask these questions in the hope that they will prompt us in this new year to express our doxology of thankfulness to God for the years he has given us in the form of a personal rededication to the Bible cause.

The UBS Identity and Ethos document approved by the Midrand Assembly (October 2000) defines our *common task* as:

achieving the widest possible, effective and meaningful distribution of the Holy Scriptures

- in languages and media which meet the needs of people world wide
- in translations that are faithful to the Scripture texts in their original languages, and which communicate the biblical message
- at prices people can afford
- and of helping people interact with the Word of God.

In this statement the three pillars are explicit; and the triple foundation is implicit.

Now back to the question: How can we reflect this ethos as a personal expression of thanks to God for his multiple goodness to us? Or, put another way, how can we lay this foundation and build these pillars in our own personalities and lifestyles?

The Pillars

Translation

The ultimate translation of the Scriptures is into life, for of all the media in today's world, none is more effective than personal lifestyle.

St Paul told the Corinthians: 'You are like a letter written by Christ and delivered by us. But you aren't written with pen and ink or on tablets made of stone. You are written in our hearts by the Spirit of the living God.' (2 Corinthians 3.3, CEV)

Let us make 2002 a year in which we daily ask the Spirit to translate the words of Christ into our lives so that these words may in turn be written in the hearts of others we will meet and get to know in the course of the year!

Distribution

How committed are we at a personal level to `achieving the widest possible, effective and meaningful distribution of the Holy Scriptures'? Are we personally (as distinct from professionally) distributing the Scriptures?

Have you ever thought of offering Scripture selections to people you meet when travelling? Or enclosing a Scripture selection with your greetings cards? Or offering an appropriate Scripture leaflet to the sick or bereaved?

Why not rehabilitate and incarnate the old word *colporteur*? It comes from the Latin `comportare' meaning to carry with one. One valid way of expressing our thanks to God would be to become a colporteur `2002 style' by always having with us some Scriptures – in audio and video formats as well as print? – for passing on to others as opportunity arises.

Engagement

Are we personally interacting with the Word of God? Are we entering the biblical narrative and becoming participants? Or, do we remain spectators?

An outstanding example of personal engagement with the Word of God is found in Luke 1.26-38. Gabriel comes to the Virgin Mary with the astounding news that she would become the mother of `the Son of the Most High God' (v.32). Mary's initial response was amazed incredulity (see v.34).

But Gabriel goes on to explain: `The Holy Spirit will come on you, and God's power will rest upon you. For this reason the holy child will be called the Son of God.... There is nothing that God cannot do.' (vv.35,37)

Then Mary's faith engages with the words of the angel: `I am the Lord's servant,' she says. `May it happen to me as you have said' (v.38). Her faith, as well as the power of the Holy Spirit, were instrumental in effecting the Incarnation!

The Word of God comes to us, as it came to Mary, as a personal message calling for our response. Why not make 2002 a year of response to, and engagement with, the Bible?

The Foundation

Prayer

The first and most basic layer in the foundation is prayer. For prayer makes things happen! Herbert Butterfield, the Oxford historian, tells us that what Christians do in prayer is more significant in shaping human history than is war or diplomacy, technology or art!

Are we attempting to work in the Bible cause – as trustees, staff, or volunteers – without having to deal with God? There is a strong temptation to do so, thanks to the power of technology and the logic of management theory. But sooner or later, we discover that we need prayer to rescue us from fatigue and anxiety, if not, also, from arrogance and pride!

God speaking through ancient texts! The Scriptures changing lives and reforming structures! For such things to happen, more is needed than the insights of Charles Handy and the creations of Bill Gates!

From his studies in the Psalms, Walter Brueggemann declares that prayer mobilises God! So let us resolve to make 2002 a year of divine mobilisation! For unless God moves, we will fail; his word will remain on the page, unable to enter human lives and transform them! And we should not be surprised if God answers our prayers by mobilising *us*! When we make the `ask', we should be prepared to become part of the answer!

Volunteerism

Volunteerism is the next layer. Without volunteers much Bible work would simply not take place! This has never been more true than today when volunteers are becoming difficult to recruit. But we thank God that in 2002 there are those who continue to be willing to deny themselves to serve others through the Bible cause.

A special word for Bible Society and UBS staff may be relevant here! The key to recruiting volunteers is to be a volunteer oneself! You cannot expect someone to respond to your invitation to give up some of their spare time to serve the Bible cause if you yourself serve it on a strictly `working hours' basis!

The same principle applies to the management of volunteers. Volunteers respond well when they are led from the front; they tend to drift away when commanded from the rear!

Our thankfulness to Christ for his faithfulness over the years can be expressed by going beyond the call of duty and becoming a Bible Society volunteer!

Fundraising

Fundraising is a vital part of the UBS foundation, as, indeed, it is of all Christian work. Encouraging people to donate money for the work of Scripture translation, distribution and engagement is the responsibility, not only of fundraisers, but also of all of us involved in the Bible Society movement.

I believe that all of us who are Bible Society or UBS staff should also be Bible Society donors! Otherwise our fundraising appeals will lack authenticity. For if we ourselves fail to support the Bible cause it is unlikely that we will be able to inspire others to do so.

131

And this also holds, in my view, for Board members. A Board member who is not also a donor is an anachronism. For someone who does not sufficiently believe in a cause to support it from their own resources, is surely unlikely to contribute to sound governance decisions on behalf of that cause. And the experience of many charitable (or, not-for-profit) organisations is that board members have great potential to become key fundraisers by quietly persuading their peers and associates in the outside world to give to the Bible Society.

So a further way to be thankful to God at the beginning of 2002 is to make this a year of thank offering! A year in which we will regularly give tangible thanks to God for his Word both by ourselves giving to the Bible cause and persuading others to do likewise.

Bible Societies and the Churches

Any reflection on incarnating the UBS ethos would be deficient without some reference to the churches. For the Midrand document states:

> The Bible Societies seek to carry out their task in partnership and cooperation with all Christian churches and with church related organisations.

So any personal recommitment to the Bible cause will necessarily involve a recommitment to serve our church. We need to take care lest we make the Bible Society or the UBS a surrogate church! Our service to the Bible cause is no substitute for active participation in the church. The Bible Society may be a house, but it's not a spiritual home! So, in this new year I appeal to all of us to find a true spiritual home in our local church where we will be regularly envisioned and empowered for the work to which God has called us.

February 2002   FAREWELL

This is my last monthly letter to you all. As you are already aware, I retire on 1 March.

On this occasion my first duty must be to thank all of you very sincerely for your steadfast support over the past four years. This I have enormously appreciated. For me, it has been a fantastic privilege to serve you during a time when the UBS transitioned from the 20th century into the 21st and successfully navigated the stormy seas of organisational change into the calmer waters of renewed trust and re-focussed mission. I have found the interaction with both Bible Societies and UBS Committees and Boards to be very stimulating, and I want to say 'Thank you ' for all you've taught me. I look forward to building on this most recent occupational learning experience in the Scripture engagement research program I hope to undertake over the next three to four years.

I want my farewell message to the Fellowship to be what the writer to the Hebrews calls a 'word of exhortation' (Hebrews 13.22). And, taking my cue from him (or was it her?) I have chosen the theme: 'Go forward together!' I am confident that the coming years will be full of great potential for Bible work, and it is my prayer that, under new leadership, our Fellowship may increase the size and multiply the impact, of its vital ministry in Scripture translation, distribution and engagement.

A world in ferment

The coming years promise to be a period of accelerated change in virtually all sections of society in nearly all the world's countries. Western culture – which, for better or for worse, is becoming universal through the influence of the mass media – especially is in ferment. The assumptions of *modernity* (reason is supreme, universal truth can be discovered, etc.) which have underpinned the political, social and scientific developments of the past 300 years, are being challenged increasingly by *post-modernity* ('Does it feel good?' replaces 'Is it true?') At the same time, the fruits of the technology which has become the driver of western culture are multiplying with bewildering rapidity, especially in electronics. There are so many changes taking place at such extraordinary speed that many people feel disoriented and confused. It is as if the 'stable' world we thought we knew has become a giant liquidiser (or blender), churning its multiple contents until they become thoroughly mixed up.

A principal, if not the primary, accelerator of this ferment is what social commentators call the 'globalisation' of the world's media and markets. Despite the anti-World Trade Organisation street protests of Seattle and Genoa, the signs are that globalisation is set to speed up rather than slow down.

One significant result of this cultural ferment is a revival of spiritualities. Millions of people, feeling threatened by so many uncertainties, are personalising and radicalising what had hitherto appears to have been a nominal religious affiliation. For evidence, look at the revival of fundamentalism in Islam, Christianity, Hinduism and Buddhism. Others are trying New Age therapies or practising neo-pagan rituals. Spirituality has become fashionable! Of course, many of the world's institutions may well remain secularised, but there is no doubt that increasing numbers of people are reacting against the secularisation of life by embracing religious fundamentalism or exploring religious pot-pourri.

This world in ferment is the world in which the UBS is called to fulfil its mission!

A movement in focus

Confronted by a world in ferment, the challenge facing the UBS will be to renew and maintain focus on its mission. That mission has recently been sharpened and clarified by the Midrand Assembly, and is well articulated in the *UBS Identity and Ethos* document. So, for the moment at least, the need for mission definition is met. The challenge of the immediate future will be how to execute this mission in our rapidly changing world. The *Direction from Midrand* identifies fifteen key strategic directions for the next few years. These are now in process of being developed into strategic programs by national Bible Societies, as well as by the Global and Area boards.

But a spiritual, as well as a strategic, response to the challenge will be required. And it is in this area that I would like to base my final message to you. For Bible work is at heart spiritual. It involves communicating the Word of God, which is much more than producing and marketing products. Of course, I expect the UBS will continue to utilise computer typesetting, project planning and a host of other technical and management know-how. But, without the Spirit's empowering of all of these tools, the UBS will sadly fail to accomplish its mission!

How might the UBS facilitate such spiritual empowerment, so necessary for moving forward together? Allow me to make three suggestions.

Hearing God speak

First, cultivate a corporate listening to the Holy Scriptures.

Contextualise the Scriptures in the strategies! Live the text in the tactics! Immerse your corporate life in the Word of God! The most effective form of Bible Society advocacy of Scripture engagement is surely to practise it!

Such hearing will enable you to `know what to do and the best time to do it' (1 Chronicles 12.32, GNB). The Scriptures are like spectacles – they help us to discern more clearly the activity of God in the world. And clear observation and analysis are an essential prelude to developing the effective future strategies which will be needed to achieve aims like the following...

> - To reflect in the composition of UBS personnel the shift of the world church's centre of gravity from the north to the south.

- To contribute to the biblical renewal of the western churches by developing helps for readers, hearers and viewers coming to the Scriptures with a post-modern mindset.

- To discover the most appropriate ways of redefining national Bible Society autonomy in the light of increasing inter-dependence in our globalised world.

- To develop strategies to ensure that the UBS ministry will benefit when the coincidence of church growth and national economic growth in the next 10-20 years will give China the potential to become a leading major net contributor to the World Service Program..

Helping Christ build

Second, keep your focus on helping Christ build his Church today and tomorrow.

I hope that the Bible Societies and the UBS in the coming years will repeatedly affirm their commitment to serve all churches and other organisations which facilitate the churches' mission. Christ is building his Church now, as at the beginning, through his disciples telling others who the Son of Man is (Matthew 16.13-20). And your privilege will be to continue to help both Christ and his 21st century disciples.

May Christ increasingly use the Bible Society family to accelerate and deepen his Church's growth, by providing human needs focused Scriptures which church members will find useful when witnessing to others!

Remember that your task in evangelism is to be a supplier, partner and catalyst to the churches, not a substitute! Maintain a genuinely inter-confessional profile, serving all churches and becoming hostage to none.

Your allegiance ultimately is to Christ, the Head of the Church (Ephesians 4.15). Make your service to the churches an expression of your commitment to him as your common Lord and Saviour. He has promised to be with you (Matthew 28.19,20). Allow him to inspire you as you…

- Challenge flagging churches to renew their commitment to fulfil the Great Commission and obey the Great Commandment.

- Design and make available to the churches, Scripture programs which will communicate hope and cultivate faith among the tragic victims of the HIV/AIDS epidemic.

- Provide churches located in the midst of TAZI audiences with Scripture programs which will enable them to use sensitively and effectively the unique tool kit of UBS TAZI Scripture resources.

135

- Seek creative ways of engaging the growing number of 'post-denominational' churches, inviting them to participate fully in the Bible Society movement.

Letting the Spirit speak

Third, be open to the leading of the Spirit.

Jesus gave the Spirit in order to lead his disciples into the true path (John 16.12-15). Bear in mind that, although the Bible is our guide, it is not an encyclopaedia containing specific answers to every problem or challenge we may come across. There are many issues in the everyday life of a Bible Society which the Scriptures do not address directly. It is to show us the way in such cases (and others) that Christ has given us his Spirit. That is why individuals and organisations that cultivate a biblical spirituality have a key advantage as they move into the future.

So I say to all of you, seek and follow the leading the Holy Spirit at all levels: governance, management, program implementation. Ask the Spirit to influence the mental processes of your individual Board members and staff, and also to guide the interaction of the people involved in your corporate planning and operational activities. May the Spirit enable the UBS family to find breakthroughs in areas which up until now have been difficult, such as…

- Maximising the potential of Bible Societies for expanding Scripture programs and raising financial resources, especially those serving the rapidly growing churches in the southern hemisphere.

- Discovering effective ways of communicating the Word of God to children and youth, who compose such a high proportion of the population in many countries and constitute the churches' most strategic audience.

- Finding cost-effective ways of developing media Scriptures for the 5 out of 10 people who don't read books.

- Developing satisfactory models of partnerships with agencies engaged in holistic ministries in ways which will enable churches to unite more effectively *kerygma* and *diakonia* in their witness.

Conclusion

Go forward together! As you do, my prayer for UBS is that it may become …

- an acoustic community hearing and obeying the voice of God in the Holy Scriptures

- a service agency effectively facilitating the churches as God's primary instrument for mission

- a spiritual odyssey continually seeking and crossing new frontiers to accomplish its vital task.

I am sure that this is also your prayer for the future. Let us all continually offer it to God in the name of Jesus, conscious that the future of the world is determined by his death, resurrection and ascension!

I can think of no better final word to leave with you than the blessing of Ephesians 5.23-24:

> **Peace be to the whole community, and love with faith, from God the Father and the Lord Jesus Christ.**
> **Grace be with all who have an undying love for our Lord Jesus Christ.** (NRSV)

Last month I received this blessing from the China Christian Council in Beijing, inscribed in beautiful Chinese caligraphy. May it be impressed on all our hearts in the attractive caligraphy of the Holy Spirit!

Appendix 1: MISSION IMPOSSIBLE?
Bible Work as Common Witness of the Churches[1]

The Holy Scriptures are the possession of all the churches. For this reason in fulfilling their mission of translating and publishing the Word of God, the Bible Societies are ready to serve all churches.

The purpose statement of the United Bible Societies indicates that `their common task of achieving the widest possible, effective and meaningful distribution of the Holy Scriptures and of helping people interact with the Word of God' is carried out `in partnership with all Christian churches and with church-related organisations.'

Strategic alliances are a common feature of the modern business world. There is a sense in which UBS member Bible Societies have been well ahead of commercial enterprises, because for many years now they have operated through a series of tacit strategic alliances with a wide spectrum of churches.

Those strategic alliances are vital to the work and witness of the Bible Societies. Without them Bible Society work would be very different from what it is. It is precisely because such alliances have been built, are being built and will be built, that it is possible to answer in the negative the question of our title.

This partnership between the churches and the Bible Societies has a three-fold foundation:

1 A Common Text

Yes, the Bible belongs to all the churches. And it also belongs to the Bible Societies. We all – churches and Bible Societies – accept it as the grand narrative which gives meaning and direction to life. For us it is the functioning story of the world.

We need constantly to remind ourselves that the Bible is fundamentally a story, a narrative, rather than a book of ideas. This is easy to forget, especially here in Europe where abstract theological thinking is so strong in the churches. The fact that the literature of the Bible is essentially narrative creates common ecumenical ground. Because, while there may be differences over the meaning or the interpretation of the story in our various ecclesiastical traditions and theological schools of thought, there is substantial agreement on the plot, the theme, the storyline of the Bible.

---

[1] Substance of a talk given in Helsinki on 5 May 1997 to church leaders at a meeting held under the auspices of the Finnish Bible Society. The quotations from the UBS Bylaws are taken from the text agreed at the Midrand World Assembly in 2000 rather than in the slightly different form of words obtaining at the time this address was given.

Inter-confessional translation and distribution projects underline that this sacred story is God's gift to all. And perhaps the role of the Bible Societies over the past two hundred years as the custodians of the text of Scripture on behalf of the churches is also a reminder that no one church holds copyright on the Word of God.

The Bible as a common text belongs primarily to all the people of God. And because the Bible is the book for all it addresses us in a translated text – unless we are native speakers of the biblical languages! It is because the Bible is for everyone that translation is such an important element in the Bible Societies' mission. Christianity, unlike Islam and many other faiths, has no sacred language. According to the gospel, God learns our language; so we don't need to learn his! This is also why Scripture translation dignifies all receptor languages. Lamin Sanneh of Yale University has testified to how the translation of the Holy Scriptures has enhanced the indigenous cultures of West Africa by making their languages the vehicle of the Word of God.

In our world where over 2 billion people are illiterate and an increasing number of television and video viewers are becoming functional post-literates, Bible Societies are placing more emphasis on translating the Scriptures into non-print media, especially the audio and the visual.

2 A Common Task

One of the primary tasks (indeed, some say *the* primary task) of the church is to proclaim, to communicate the Word of God.

There is an overlap here with the reference in the purpose statement of UBS to 'effective and meaningful distribution', because Scripture distribution cannot be either effective or meaningful unless the churches communicate the Word to the people of God and, through them, to the world.

The story is not Good News unless and until it is told! This is why neither the churches nor the Bible Societies can accept the privatisation of Scripture which our secularised and post-modern world wishes upon us. We are often told that we may have the gospel as long as we keep it to ourselves. But if we keep it to ourselves it is not the gospel!

It is through communicating the story that it becomes alive. As people hear it they find themselves enabled by the Holy Spirit to indwell it and make the story their own. And they discover the meaning of their existence and the meaning of the universe.

Churches and Bible Societies have complementary roles in fulfilling this common task of telling God's Story. While the churches are the sowers of the Good Seed, the Bible Societies are the seed merchants. As such, the Bible Societies serve the churches. They are not, however, 'owned' by any one denomination or confession. Bible Societies serve the churches – yes! But their service is like that of African jungle guides. Sometimes they walk behind carrying the bags; at others they go ahead to find the way. But when Bible Societies go ahead they always act as catalysts to the churches and not as substitutes for them.

3 A Common Testimony

All over the world churches of differing traditions are finding that distributing together a gospel portion, or a shorter Scripture selection, is an effective common act of Christian witness. This common commitment to sowing the Good Seed means that in many countries the Bible Society achieves a wide range of ecumenical cooperation that many other bodies find impossible.

Common Scripture distribution has been most effective where the people of God are mobilised to share their faith with others, for person-to-person contexts provide the sense of community which is the social context of good communication.

Mobilising the people of God to witness to others about Jesus Christ with the help of a Scripture portion or selection has never been more appropriate than in our post-modern era where people are very open to story but very suspicious of ideas. Reynold Price argues that the need for *homo sapiens* to tell and hear stories is second only to the need for nourishment! 'We crave nothing less than perfect story: and while we chatter or listen all our lives in a din of craving – jokes, anecdotes, novels, dreams, films, plays, songs, half the words of our days – we are satisfied only by the one short tale we feel to be true: History is the will of a just God who knows us.' (*A Palpable God*)

Perhaps the reason why people are today becoming particularly open to story is that we have arrived at the frontier between the modern and the post-modern worlds. Thomas Oden puts this paradigm shift into historical context when he says that the modern age came into existence in 1789 with the storming of the Bastille, and came to an end with the fall of the Berlin Wall in 1989. Historical and cultural periods of transition often create new attitudes of openness which both churches and Bible Societies do well to take advantage of!

Common witness is more than something churches and Bible Societies do together. Our witness is common also because our respective testimony has a common subject – Jesus Christ. He is both the subject and (in a sense) the author of the story. That is why he, unlike other historical characters, can – as Luther put it – step out of the page to meet us. Ultimately it is he who makes effective and meaningful the witness of both our churches and our Bible Societies.

Common witness is not without its challenges. Bible Societies are often too nervous to take bold initiatives. And churches, for their part, tend to be so self-absorbed that they often see Bible work as an option to be taken up only after they have solved all their problems!

But common witness *is* possible! And in an increasing number of countries and localities it is becoming a powerful reality. Harold Goddard reminds us that all stories are powerful. 'The destiny of the world', he claims, 'is determined less by the battles that are lost and won than by the stories it loves to believe in.' (*The Making of Shakespeare*). Surely this general observation is particularly true of the biblical story, for it is the power of God for salvation to everyone who has faith' (Romans 1.16).

Appendix 2: REBUILDING TRUST[1]

In September 1997 the UBS Executive Committee passed the following resolutions:
* To note the General Secretary's comments on trust and ask the UBSEC Chairman and UBS President to develop a plan of action to deal with the situation.
* To request both the retiring and the new General Secretaries to make the re-establishment of a high level of trust throughout the UBS Fellowship a top priority.

The purpose of this report is to open a debate among members of UBSEC about the lead UBSEC might give to the Fellowship to encourage all of us to resolve the issue of trust identified in these resolutions. For if we are to rebuild trust we first need to lay a strong foundation.

I believe that right at the beginning of this debate we have to face the hard question: 'Why did the breakdown of trust occur?'

I have put this question to several people who know our Fellowship well and I have received many answers. One of the most startling was: 'Because we have become worldly.' At first this sounds simplistic and pietistic. But the more I have thought of it, the more I have come to the conclusion that we need to consider very seriously whether this observation is true.

Wrestling with the charge that the UBS has become a worldly organisation, I have found two recent publications very helpful. The first is the Oct. 1997 issue of *The International Review of Mission*, published by the Conference on World Mission and Evangelism of the WCC. The other is Dr Eugene Habecker's recent book *Rediscovering the Soul of Leadership*.

Trends which undermine trust

That issue of the *IRM* is devoted to considering approaches to a missionary agenda into the next century. Following the Conference on World Mission and Evangelism in Salvador, Brazil, in 1996, it identifies the principle features of the contemporary secular context in the following four clusters of issues:
* Globalisation
* Postmodernity
* Fragmentation
* Religious Plurality[2]

---

[1] General Secretary's Report to UBS Executive Committee, Iguacu, Brazil: March 31-April 2 1988.

[2] It is important to distinguish between plurality and pluralism. Plurality presupposes a whole, thus in terms of Christianity it affirms the catholicity of the church and of the Christian faith. Pluralism, on the other hand, makes a principle out of fragmentation into differing views, emphasizes the subjective validity or each of them and, this way, loses sight of the whole.' (*IRM* p.429)

It is significant that three out of these four trends undermine trust!

Globalisation of the world's economies is converting our `global village' - created by the mass media - into a global market which encourages personal advancement over communal responsibility. Individual wants are placed above the essential needs of the community and, indeed, of humanity. As the North American television advertisement puts it: `Because if you're not the top dog, the scenery never changes'.

Postmodernity is increasingly challenging the vision of an ordered, rational world. Truth is privatised. Personal experience is taking the place of reason in knowledge and understanding. The focus is on the present moment: the past and the future don't really matter. People are persuaded that they are the real masters of their own lives, free to pick and choose whatever may advance personal achievement and private joy.

Fragmentation is `the sign of our time' (*IRM* p.393). It manifests itself ethnically in varying degrees along a spectrum ranging from the breakdown of `the melting pot' of the USA to the bloody genocides of Rwanda and Bosnia. Fragmentation is also economic: `The world is split into the consumers and the consumed' (p.400).

Globalisation... Postmodernity... Fragmentation... Signs of our time! Signs that prompt four questions:

1 Does our UBS structure contribute to globalisation? Is there enough space to celebrate our diversity within our overall unity?

2 In our marketing of Scriptures are we in danger of allowing the focus on `felt needs' of individuals to override the `essential needs' of communities? In other words, are we contributing to the current fragmentation?

3 Are there times when our national Bible Societies become nationalistic by claiming that their vision of a Bible Society is superior to that of all others?

4 Are our regional rivalries a disguised form of mega-ethnic conflict?

Simply having to face such questions makes us realise that many of the prevailing global trends mean that in the future we will have to work much harder at creating and maintaining trust than was needed in the past.

Thinking that destroys trust

Dr Habecker's book has a most helpful chapter on `Power, Authority and Trust' in which he perceptively analyses three false ways of thinking which can destroy trust in any community.

* Either/or thinking
* Hard is better than soft
* Mistrust of the world

Either/or thinking assumes that only two primary options exist for any decision. Any consideration of multiple - even plural - solutions to problems is swept aside. The range of options for resolving difficulty is quickly reduced to two which soon become symbols of polarisation.

Hard is better than soft thinking assumes automatically that in making decisions hard facts or firm numbers are superior to feelings or intuition.

Mistrust of the world thinking assumes the world is a dangerous place in which only the fittest and the mistrusting survive. It is the mentality which says: `I need to get the other person before that person gets me. Our organisation needs to come up with the creative plan or program first; otherwise, our competitor will take away all our potential gift income.'

Again, this analysis prompts us to ask some hard questions:

1   At the next World Assembly will we trust the Assembly sufficiently to consider multiple strategy options?

2   Does the male dominance of Bible Society leadership (Board and staff) make us a less trusting organisation? Women are more intuitive than men. And Dr Habecker reminds us that `trust appears to be a soft variable' (p.37).

3   Have we become so suspicious of the competition for the donors' dollar that we now find it more difficult to trust our fellow UBS members?

The challenge facing us is to build a global Fellowship of trust which has to work in an untrusting world where the atmosphere of distrust infiltrates our homes, our churches and our Bible Societies!

An Open Book

1 believe the first major step in responding to this challenge and building trust among ourselves is to re-kindle our trust in the Bible. Ought we to make greater efforts to live our corporate life - both in our national Bible Societies and in the UBS - out of the Bible?

When the BFBS was founded in 1804 the prevailing culture was Christian (but, of course, far from perfect!), so many of the trends in the world tended to reinforce the ethos of the Bible Society. Today it is very different! Of course the modem world is by no means entirely bad, but so much of the influence of its prevailing trends is selfish, envious and hateful. It negates - and will, if we allow it, destroy the Christian ethos of the UBS.

That is why we Bible Society people also need the Bible! The book we promote to others is also a word for us. The Word is the seed of the strong trust in God which gives us the ability to trust others.

Perhaps we need to pause more often in our enthusiasm to give the Word to others, to ask how we can rediscover its relevance for the ethos of our Bible Societies and of our beloved global Fellowship! In our committees and assemblies we face a new challenge to marry Scripture and strategy, prayer and policy. Is the UBS Executive Committee ready to give a lead?

An Open Mind

In the concluding paragraphs of his section on trust, Dr Habecker suggests trust can be built and re-built by good leadership. He says leaders who build trust do three things. Let me quote him more or less verbatim:

1 Leaders who provide and search for multiple options as potential solutions to problems or identify a variety of opportunities for the future do much to build trust in an organisation.

2 Leaders who insist on hard data but who also allow for prayer, the role of intuition, and other types of soft input, tend to end up with the most solid decisions. This is particularly true in a Christian organization which allows for and earnestly seeks the guidance of the Holy Spirit. Often God's clear leading can't be quantified.

3 And leaders who choose to take a positive view of the world and the people they lead end up looking for the best in people and situations, not the worst.
Dr Habecker concludes: `Some would argue that this sack of realism' will ultimately be in the worst interests of the leader. To the contrary, leaders who practise these three elements build trust and identify for followers multiple options for possible organizational futures.' (*Rediscovering the Soul of Leadership* p.39)

Conclusion

So we come back to our first question: 'Why did the breakdown of trust occur'?' I am convinced that the fault lies with all of us. We were overtaken unawares by the profound change of world view which has taken place over the last decade as the world has moved away from modernity towards postmodernity.

> The modern age came into existence in 1789 with the storming of the Paris Bastille, and came to an end with the fall of the Berlin Wall in 1989. (Thomas Oden)

Let me end with St Paul's advice to the Christians in Rome - what better watch word for the future?

> **Dear friends, God is good. So I beg you to offer your bodies to him as a living sacrifice, pure and pleasing. That's the most sensible way to serve God. Don't be like the people of this world, but let God change the way you think. Then you will know how to do everything that is good and pleasing to him.** (Romans 12.1-2, CEV)

Appendix 3: SCRIPTURE ENGAGEMENT[1]

In its edition of 16 April, 2000 - the first day of Holy Week - the Sunday Times Magazine of London, England, carried a cover picture of a stone replica of 'The Holy Bible' in process of disintegrating into myriads of pieces. The caption read: 'Breaking Faith: the gospel according to science'.

The accompanying article, entitled 'Digging up the Dirt on the Bible' and lavishly illustrated in full colour, was a journalistic resume of the views of Ze'ev Herzog, a professor of archaeology at Tel Aviv University. Herzog's revision of biblical texts is causing controversy in Israel, although he is by no means the first archaeologist to reconstruct the biblical story in the light of archaeological evidence or its absence.

For me, two features of this article are significant. The first is that one of the western world's most prestigious newspapers assumes that its dramatic Palm Sunday cover represents the contemporary view of the Bible. And the second is the link made in the article between 'present day Bible-bashing' views like Herzog's and 'the intellectual fashion for deconstruction'.

The Sunday Times' feature highlights the enormous challenge western churches and Bible Societies are facing in communicating the Bible, and illustrates the urgent need for both to take Scripture engagement seriously.

The challenge of Scripture engagement is also found in the non-western world, even in areas where demand for the Scriptures is incessant and distribution is high. High distribution numbers are, of course, encouraging. But they alone are not the mark of success. For only when the Scriptures distributed are used in ways which fulfill God's purpose for them can we say 'Mission accomplished'! Karl Barth used to say that the Bible does not become God's Word to us if we use it as a prop to hold up a short table leg! Similarly, Bibles used as a charm to ward off evil spirits, or as an amulet in a bride's wedding outfit, or as an ornamental volume in the family bookshelf are unlikely to result in Scripture engagement.

I think all of us in our global family agree that, as Bible Societies, we need to be concerned that the Scriptures we distribute are used, and that they are used in ways which are in line with their divine purpose. But there is less consensus on whether Bible Societies ought to take active steps to remedy the non-use or misuse of the Scriptures, for some of us tend to see this as the task of the churches.

In truth, this is surely the task of both the Bible Societies and the churches. That is not to say that the roles of both are identical. They are, in fact, complementary: while the churches help people engage with the Scriptures, the Bible Societies help the Scriptures engage with people.

---

[1] General Secretary's Report to the UBS Executive Committee, Amman, 22-26 May 2000

Bible Societies rightly continue to be reluctant to stray into the interpretative and teaching role of the churches; the most recent UBS Guidelines for Study Bibles (1992) exclude `material which imposes post-biblical doctrinal formulations, expresses the distinctive tenets of a particular denomination or theological tendency, or prescribes any specific contemporary application.' But these same Guidelines go on to state: 'The study materials, however, should be written so as to allow the readers to discover applications to their own situations.' This last sentence describes Scripture engagement.

While Scripture engagement has always been implicit in our Bible Society mission, there is no doubt that it has become more prominent in recent years. There are two basic reasons for this. They are:

- Because of where people are
- Because of what the Bible is

Where people are

In many countries people today are further removed from the Bible than they were a decade or two ago. This is true (to different degrees) of both people within, and people outside our churches.

Within many churches biblical illiteracy is high. In the UK the proportion of church members who read the Bible two or three times a week varies between 3 and 10%. In many churches the Sunday sermons consist of isolated Scripture titbits for Christian consumers who seldom get past the appetiser stage. In some churches which pride themselves in `expository ministry', the sermon becomes a mini lecture in biblical theology rather than a transposition of the biblical text's message into the 21st century.

The scene in UK churches reflects what is happening in many other western countries where the situation is frequently exacerbated by degrees of ambivalence regarding the status of the Bible in the ongoing life of the churches. This incongruity is summed up by Dan Beeby - an advisor to the Open Book project of BFBS and the English churches - when he says that `to a large extent the western church possesses a Bible but not a scripture.'

The situation in the non-western world is in some ways healthier. Bibles are sought after and highly valued. Churches are growing. But here also there is much that discourages biblical literacy. Allow me to illustrate from two recent experiences in my travels for the UBS. Last year I attended an evangelical church in Asia; during the service the Bible was not formally read and it was scarcely referred to in the sermon. I also participated recently in an African service in which the preaching was pure brilliance in terms of communication, but in no way was it an exercise in Scripture engagement. For the sermon was totally allegorical with hardly any ongoing relationship to the passage from which the preacher took his theme.

While there are people outside the churches who value the Bible highly, most non-church people are seldom exposed to the Bible because our media culture has edged it into the private sphere. So the Bible has become marginalised; it is seen as personal preference, not public truth. In the minds of many, science and technology have made God redundant and rendered the Bible surplus to requirements for everyday living.

However, the last decade has witnessed a remarkable reaction against secularisation in the form of a search for alternative spiritualities by a growing number of people who might be described as post-modern pilgrims. But so far this remarkable paradigm shift has brought little comfort to the churches or attention to the Bible, for in the eyes of many post-moderns the Bible is invalidated by the fact that Christians believe it to be the functioning story of the world.

For post-moderns there can be no master-story; each person creates their own reality and discovers their own truth. All stories, especially master-stories, are human, social constructions created by their authors to impose order on the world and dominate the masses. Many people today call for the `deconstruction' of such stories which, they claim, would have the effect of liberating those who have been suppressed by them.

Developments such as these have led some Bible Societies to lay more stress on Bible advocacy. In the 1980's the Bible Society in Australia sponsored a series of Olivier Beguin Memorial Lectures. The title of the lecture for 1985 - `The Authority and Relevance of the Bible in the Modern World' - sums up the aim of the lecture series. A more recent example is the `Open Book' initiative of the British and Foreign Bible Society in association with English churches. At last April's meeting of the Forum of Bible Agencies, David Spriggs, Head of Church Relations at BFBS, introduced this programme. He demonstrated how the advance of secularisation and the advent of postmodernism had forced the BFBS to change the focus of its home programme from the Scriptures' availability and relevance to their credibility.

The best form of advocacy of the Bible is to engage people with it. The mission statement of the `Open Book' campaign is: `Putting God's Story into the heart of the nation in our generation'. To facilitate this aim, five biblical stories have been identified.

These are: Creation, Exodus, Exile and Return, Nativity and the Cross.

The Open Book campaign is seeking to make these stories common currency once more in English culture by communicating them in a variety of media, promoting them not as church texts, but as God's Story for the whole world, and relating each of these stories to a key theme which resonates with a felt need of many people today. Thus, the Creation story is linked with identity, Exodus with freedom, the Exile and Return with justice, the Nativity with hope and the Cross with forgiveness.

To sum up so far: Scripture engagement is paramount today because the great majority of people are ignorant of the Bible's message, and even in the churches many have a superficial knowledge of it.

We now come to consider the second reason why Scripture engagement is demanding our attention: unless Scripture engages with its audience, it fails to fulfill its purpose.

What the Bible is

Today we are re-discovering the nature of the Bible as story. This re-discovery is one aspect of a new appreciation of the role of narrative in literature as a central category for understanding human life and discovering how to live ethically in the world.

When the Bible is described as story, it is not being claimed that it consists exclusively of texts in the narrative genre. Within it there is, of course, a variety of non-narrative material, such as laws, proverbs, poems, and letters. But all of this material is embedded within the framework of a grand epic which moves from creation, through fall and redemption, to new creation.

This re-discovery of Scripture as narrative is welcome. For too long the Bible had been thought of as a book of ideas, a text book of theology rather than as a literary collection. As Thomas Long has graphically put it, we have tended to throw the text of Scripture into the exegetical winepress to squeeze out the ideas! But today there is a new focus on the text itself as text.

Today there is also a growing recognition that the Bible is essentially a book for the people rather than for the specialists, a text which provides ordinary human beings with a hand book for living.

The title of the Spanish Popular Version, *Dios Habla Hoy* (God speaks today) immediately suggests that the Bible is an engaging book. And it is true that in quite remarkable ways the Holy Spirit speaks through its pages to people today of all cultures and languages into which the Bible has been translated. Such encounters with God in and through his Word are not automatic and cannot be defined scientifically. But everyone involved in Bible work knows that they occur.

This remarkable ability of the Bible to `speak' to people ought not to surprise us. Again and again, the Letter to the Hebrews quotes the Old Testament Scriptures with a phrase like `as the Holy Spirit says' - using the present tense (see 3.7,15; 10.15,17,37; and 12.5,25). Hebrews 4.12 describes the Word of God as `alive and active' and then, almost in the same breath, goes on to speak of God himself as the one before whom `all are naked and laid bare' (NRSV). (CEV: `He sees through everything, and we will have to tell him the truth'). The Word is alive and active precisely because God uses it!

The Greek word translated by the NRSV as `laid bare' is an uncommon one which was sometimes used in the ancient world of a wrestler seizing his opponent by the throat and pinning him down so that he was unable to move! What a dramatic picture! The Word of God has such critical power to confront our hypocrisy, selfishness and sheer unbelief that it is as if God himself pins us to the floor and demands a submission! Little wonder that Martin Luther observed that the Word of God comes to us as adversary as well as friend!

As we have seen, the basic infrastructure of the Bible is a narrative or story whose theme is the universal story of humanity from creation to new creation. Within this universal framework lies a covenantal dimension. The Bible comes to us in two parts: the Old Testament (or covenant) and the New Testament (or covenant). The word covenant expresses a special relationship between God and his people. One of the particular forms of covenant in ancient near eastern culture which was borrowed by biblical writers to describe God's relationship with his people was that covenant made between a great king (or emperor) and a vassal king. Biblical scholars have detected this type of covenant framework in some key parts of the Old Testament, such as Deuteronomy.

So the Bible is a story which is told with a view to creating and maintaining a relationship between God and us. This is why when we read or hear the biblical story we are invited to enter the story and indwell it.

We should point out that Luther's description of the Word of God as adversary does not negate the Good News! In fact the great translator laid greater stress on the other side of the coin, for he used to say that Jesus Christ steps out of the Scriptures to meet us as we read and hear them. The history of the Bible Society movement over almost two centuries confirms that engagement with Scripture leads to encounter with Christ. This should not surprise us, for Jesus himself taught that the Scriptures witness to him (John 5.39).

We read that the risen Christ, on meeting with the two disciples on the road to Emmaus, `opened to them the Scriptures'. Some think this metaphor suggests that Christ opened the door into the Scriptures and invited the disciples to enter. And he invited them to enter the story in order that they might understand the tragedy which was so preoccupying them at the time. In fact Christ helped them infer from the story that the tragedy was the pivot to which the story pointed. This engagement with the Scriptures brought light into the disciples' darkened world and caused their hearts to burn within them.

In some ways Scripture engagement is still like this today. It involves accepting God's invitation to enter the story, to become part of it and to submit ourselves to it. It also means inferring from it what God wants us to do at this particular point in our lives, or in our week, or in our day.

To sum up this section: the Bible is God's Story which he wants us to tell to the world. It's a story he invites us to enter in order that we might hear him speak to us, inviting us into an intimate relationship with himself. Unless the Bible impacts individuals and communities in this way, it fails to fulfill the purpose God has for it.

The Bible scratches where people itch

Before reviewing some models of Scripture engagement which are particularly useful today, I want briefly to highlight that the re-discovery of the significance of the Bible as story in itself provides us with a key resource in communicating its message to our contemporaries who have discarded it.

First of all, the Bible as story relates admirably to the current popularity of story telling as a primary means of communication.

Second, the Bible' story line - especially the strong Old Testament focus on the desert wanderings and the Babylonian exile - resonates remarkably with the spiritual pilgrimage of many people today in our postmodern world.

Third, the Bible's keen sensitivity to suffering demonstrates its particular relevance to a very similar sensitivity among many 21st century post-Christian people.

Fourth, the courage to doubt, evident in many of the psalms, echoes the acute moral dilemmas faced by many people today who are acutely aware of injustice in the world, but who want to believe in a God who is good and loving.

Looking at these four remarkable correspondences between the Bible and contemporary felt needs and moods, one is tempted to conclude that if only a point of contact could be found where the horizon of the biblical text of Scripture could intersect with the horizon of people today, the result would be an extraordinary revival of interest in the Bible!

However, to get people today into Scripture we require helps which will not only offer information about the text, but also invite users of Scripture to engage with it. Such helps will, in effect, be prompts to Scripture engagement. At the moment UBS Study Bibles guidelines focus largely on helps relating to language, literary genre, culture and history. Essentially they provide information which is implicit in the text and which would have been readily apparent to the original readers and hearers. But is this enough in the early 21st century? Almost certainly not! My impression is that our UBS Study Bibles - however excellent they may be in terms of the prescribed criteria - are not the first choice (where there is a choice) of many who wish to engage with the text as distinct from analysing it.

But the inevitable question arises: can we extend our range of helps in this way without straying into the interpretative, magisterial role of the Churches in relation to Scripture? I believe it is possible to move the text of Holy Scripture nearer today's readers without infringing the ministry of the churches. In fact, Bible Societies may be uniquely positioned to build such bridges between text and people in the light of the evidence we have already noted of the alienation of many people from the churches and the failure of many churches to engage the faithful with the Word.

Helps toward Scripture engagement

I believe that the following models of Scripture engagement have great potential to help us achieve a breakthrough among people of the 21" century.

1 Meditation

As Psalm 119 affirms, Scripture is designed to be meditated upon. But the pace of modem living often makes this difficult, and we ignore this form of engagement.

> Meditation on Scripture creates specially favorable conditions for God to speak to us in it and through it, and evoke our response of loving attention, gratitude, of pain, desire, caring, offering, questioning, repenting, trusting, letting go, promising, or whatever it may be.
>
> - Martin L Smith in his helpful book *The Word is very near you: A guide to praying with Scripture*, p.45.

As the title of his book suggests, Smith believes strongly in combining meditation with prayer.

> Meditative prayer with Scripture is the art of absorbing, taking in image after image of Scripture so that the Spirit within us can impress the deepest levels of our being with their meaning. In meditative prayer the Spirit makes the connection between our deepest needs and the images that answer them and convey the grace and touch of God's power.. (p.45).

Martin Smith also underlines the importance of meditating as we attempt to enter biblical stories. 'Jesus used parables to provoke a crisis in the faith of the hearer. The use of parables demanded that the listeners enter into the stories, experience them from the inside, give up normal, conventional responses and allow the flow of the narrative to take them into a new, strange insight where they had never been before.' (p.92f) He provides helpful guidelines for meditating with events in the biblical Story (pp.105-7), as well as for meditating on didactic texts (pp.119-121).

Today a growing number of people many people are coming to recognise the spiritual barrenness of busy lives and are consciously making more time for reflection. In the light of this, is today a *kairos* to introduce prompts to meditation in the helps we offer?

2 Transposition

I well remember being introduced to biblical transpositions shortly after I was appointed General Secretary of the National Bible Society of Scotland in 1981. I attended an `introduction week' for new Bible Society staff organised by the regional service centre which was then located in London. The highlight of the week for me was the Bible studies led by Paul Fueter, the regional Distribution Consultant.

Paul helped us to open up specific passages of Scripture by employing the technique of transposition - i.e. transposing the message of the text into another medium, whether drama, poster, poetry or music. I'll never forget making a poster which sought to portray the message of reconciliation in Christ of Jew (`us') and Gentile (`you') contained in Ephesians 2 and 3. Paul demonstrated to us that approaching the Bible for communication rather than consumption enabled us to discover new truths previously missed. A few months later I had the opportunity of working on the same passage with a group of Presbyterian young people in Northern Ireland and rejoiced in the way they designed and produced their posters to challenge the sectarian divisions of Irish society.

I believe that by introducing into our helps challenges to transpose biblical texts in simple ways into other media will not only enable today's readers to discover new insights and fresh relevance from the passage, but that it will also encourage them to share the biblical message with others.

3 Improvisation

One particular form of transposition is drama. A particularly effective way of dramatising Scripture as a group activity is to get the group to re-enact biblical passages and to interrupt the drama abruptly just before the climax. Then the group is asked: 'What would you do if you were Daniel or Mary Magdalene, etc.?'

Richard Middleton and Brian Walsh following N T Wright (*Truth is stranger than it used to be*), have recently provided a rationale for a dramatic approach by breaking the Bible narrative into six acts, each with multiple scenes, as follows:
- Act I   Story of Creation
- Act II   Story of the Fall.
- Act III   Story of Israel
- Act IV   Story of Jesus
- Act V   Story of the Church
- Act VI   The Eschaton or consummation

Middleton and Walsh emphasise that the script breaks off in Act V. There is a gap between Act V, scene 1 (the story of the early church) and the climactic finale of the drama in Act VI depicted in the Book of Revelation. We are in real life among the actors in Act V, for our response to the biblical text is to work out new scenes in the Fifth Act, and in this way carry forward the God's Story today in ways which are faithful to the biblical story line. This involves immersing ourselves in the Scriptures in order to get to know the story line really well. Such improvisation also calls for creative, innovative and flexible thinking and action.

The improvised continuation of the biblical story in our lives and situations can be greatly facilitated by the dramatic re-enactment of specific passages. Could this technique be incorporated into our study Bibles by flagging points in the text where it might be appropriate to `cut' the drama and ask: `What would you do?'

4 Imagination

Another category of helps we should consider for readers and hearers of the Scriptures concerns providing stimuli to their imagination which will encourage them to indwell the story. If helps are exclusively scientific they will encourage detached analysis of the text rather than personal absorption in it. We need to learn to take in what a biblical passage says before we ask what it means. Simply because the Bible is story, it is vital that we take time as we read it and hear it to become absorbed in the story line.

Today biblical scholars are re-discovering the importance of the role of imagination in engaging with Scripture. The Bible's literary forms are seen as much more than mere packaging for the ideas lying behind the words. There is greater stress on the text as text and on the power of the different literary genres to shape our thinking and living. `The biblical texts are concerned not only to teach truth by means of logical propositions, but to display the truth to the whole person with a veritable arsenal of imaginative communicative strategies.' (*Biblical Literature and Literary Criticism*, a presentation by Kevin Vanhoozer to The National Bible Society of Scotland, 1990.)

Martin Smith offers the following advice on how to enter the biblical Story. After reading the text slowly and carefully several times, pausing between readings to note the details: `Place the Bible aside. Now give your power of imagination free rein to bring the scene to life with yourself as a participant. Don't look at it as if it were a movie projected onto a screen. It is happening all around you. Feel absolutely free to smell the scents of seashore and marketplace. Hear the noises, sense the movements. Allow yourself to become whoever you want in the scene. Are you one of the disciples? A bystander able to see everything happen right there on the spot? Are you the sick person? If so, how are you feeling at the beginning of the story?' (p. 106).

When we read a novel or watch a film we allow ourselves to get involved in the plot, and often it is only afterwards that we ask what it all means. For some strange reason we tend to reverse this process when approaching the Bible: unless we can understand it we don't want to get involved! Perhaps this is due to the scientific conditioning of hi-tech society with its virtual reality which is increasingly robbing us of the ability to read and hear imaginatively.

Do we need to introduce appropriate imagination prompts to our list of helps? Why not include in Study Bibles an introductory article offering some basic suggestions for narrative, poetry, parable, wisdom literature, etc. One suggestion for `inhabiting' a narrative passage could be: `Imagine yourself as a television journalist sent to prepare a news report on the incident(s) described. Interview the characters in the story to probe their motives and attitudes to the other characters. Or, interview the writer about his objectives and the means he uses to achieve them. Or, conduct a survey among the first hearers of the story and prepare a popular resume of their reactions.'

5 Interrogation

We have already noted that our UBS Study Bible Guidelines indicate that the study materials provided `should be written so as to allow the readers to discover applications to their own situations.' These guidelines were developed originally through a dialogue held in the Europe and the Middle East Region between publishers and translation consultants. As a participant in that dialogue, I had a hand in drafting the guidelines. But I now wonder whether we employed the best verb. Today I would want to go a little further by using `to encourage' rather than `to allow,' for engagement between text and reader is ultimately what Bible work is all about, and we should enthusiastically advocate it.

On the other hand, the guidelines rightly exclude `material which... prescribes any specific contemporary application.' This exclusion not only keeps Bible Societies from straying into the rightful role of the churches; it is also very much in line with the post-modern preference for options and dislike of prescriptions.

A key method of encouraging applications of biblical passages to contemporary situations by readers, hearers and viewers is by offering them some contextualising questions they themselves can put to the text. In this way the answers are discovered by them, not prescribed by others. The questions should enable users to build bridges from the passage to themselves. Questions could be standard, applicable to any passage of Scripture, or they could be passage-specific. Some Bible agencies already employ such standard questions. For example, Scripture Union include the following standard questions in some of its reading plans.

- What have you read about God, Jesus or the Holy Spirit?
- In these verses is there...
  a command to obey?
  a promise to believe?
  a good example to follow?
  a wrong thing to avoid?

Alternatively (or additionally), questions which are passage-specific can be used. For example, the following questions could be applied to the story of the exodus from Egypt (Exodus 12.37-14.31):

1 Do we really look to God as liberator?

2 Do we hear God saying today to those who keep other human beings in political, social and economic bondage, `Let my people go'?

3. On whose side do we stand regarding the oppression of the weak by the powerful in our own day?

4. What was the exodus which Luke's gospel tells us Jesus was to accomplish at Jerusalem? (See Luke 9.30,31)

An additional and significant advantage for the Bible Societies asking questions of the text is that it enables us to engage people in interpreting the text without us adopting a position one doctrinal or ethical interpretation over against another. It is true, of course, that the selection of the questions might reflect distinct interpretations, but steps can be taken to avoid any serious offense being taken by church traditions and schools of biblical scholarship.

6 Interaction

Another type of help begins with the felt needs of particular audiences and moves from the need to the text. This approach is often used very effectively in selections and portions which focus on a specific issue. I have recently seen an excellent selection on AIDS from the Bible Society in Chile and a superb portion on the same subject from the Bible Society of South Africa.

Such helps are found in some non-UBS study Bibles. One of the most effective use of this approach is in the New Century Youth Bible where the helps highlight a key issue for young people. One key issue is resisting the wrong kind of peer pressure (at Psalm 1); another dealing with hero worship (at Acts 14.8-20). The help contains an anecdotal illustration from today's world, and then goes on to ask readers to discover what the text has to say to them about these issues.

The New Century Youth Bible reflects a particular stance in biblical interpretation, which would not be open to Bible Societies to adopt. However, the strength of many of its helps is independent of the publisher's theological stance, and rests on an invitation to move from a felt need into the text and back to the felt need. I see no good reason why Bible Societies should not, with care, follow such an interactive approach. We already do so with selections. Is there any reason in principle why we cannot do something similar in study Bibles?

Conclusion

All six types of `helps towards Scripture engagement' which we have reviewed involve essentially right brain activities. They stimulate the intuitive and creative areas of our personalities. As such they differ from the analytical and informative helps which engage the left side of our brain and, which - so far - constitute the class of helps offered in our UBS Study Bibles.

Because the analytical and scientific approach to knowledge is deeply distrusted by a growing section of the public, our traditional helps have become significantly less useful than they were, say, a decade ago. This is why we must consider supplementing these traditional annotations with the kind of helps we have reviewed, especially as the post-modern world is more open to intuitive and inductive methods of learning.

BIBLE INDEX

156

2.14-16	62
3.3	129
4.4	14
5.16-18	80
8.2	112-3
8.4	94, 113
8.9	113
8.12	112
9.7	113
9.8,11	112
9.13	94

Galatians
3.2	72
3.28	66
4.4	50-51

Ephesians
1.7	31
1.19-20	6
2.14	107, 151
2.19	11
4.13	51
4.15	135
5.2	62
5.22-24	66, 137
5.26	76

Philippians
1.21	60
2.5-7	107
2.6-11	174
3.10	29
3.14	9
3.20	11
4.1-3	66
4.8	113
4.18	62

Colossians
1.15	14
1.16-17	31
4.5-6	35

1 Thessalonians
1.2-3	5
1.5-6	3
2.1-10	3
2.17	4
4.8	3
5.13-14	4
5.18-19	3

2 Thessalonians
3.1	2

1 Timothy
2.8-15	66

2 Timothy
1.7	5
2.1-7	101f

Hebrews
1.1	50-51
3.7,15	148
4.12-13	148
10.15,17,37	148
11.3	86
12.5,25	148
13.22	133

James
4.14	119

1 Peter
1.3	97
1.15-16	69
2.21	127
3.1-6	66

1 John
1.6	90
2.9	120
2.10-11	90
4.2-10	50

Revelation
1.2	53
1.18	53
3.14	53
5.8	54
5.9	71
7.9	71
8.3-5	54
12.9	53
13.14	53
14.6	71
18.23	53
19.11	53
20.1-10	52-54
21.4	54
22.6	53
22.1-2,19	38